"Anosh Irani has crafted a story as black and seductive as a desert night."
—*The Globe and Mail*

"Excellent characterization and humour bring [this] cruel drama to life."
—*The Vancouver Sun*

"...raunchy yet elegant... an engaging exploration of the darker side of human nature."
—*The Westender*

"Top Rani's desire to understand his sexuality is very powerful. And this is perhaps where east meets west in Irani's intriguing play."
—*Vancouver Courier*

BOMBAY BLACK

Winner of 4 Dora Mavor Moore Awards including: Outstanding New Play, Outstanding Set Design, Costume Design, and Sound Design/Composition. Nominations for Outstanding Production and Lighting Design.

"Sensuous, lyrical, mysterious, sordid, grotesque, romantic and highly emblematic..."
—*The Globe and Mail*

"Pungent and lyrical and sometimes witty. Line by line, Irani never hits a false note."
—*National Post*

"Playwright Anosh Irani carefully navigates between convincing casual conversation and rich lyricism... a precarious balance between beautiful mythology and ugly realism, between hope and despair."
—*Eye Weekly*, ****

"Anosh Irani's sultry, spooky and surreal tale of thwarted love and bittersweet revenge... beautifully captures the optimism of love against all odds."
—*NOW Magazine*, NNNN

The Bombay Plays

The Matka King
Bombay Black

THE BOMBAY PLAYS

THE MATKA KING
BOMBAY BLACK

Anosh Irani

Playwrights Canada Press
Toronto • Canada

PLAYWRIGHTS CANADA PRESS
202-269 Richmond St. W., Toronto, ON M5V 1X1
416.703.0013 • info@playwrightscanada.com • www.playwrightscanada.com

For amateur or professional production rights, please contact:
The Gary Goddard Agency
149 Church Street, 2nd Floor
Toronto, ON M5B 1Y4
416-928-0299, meaghan@garygoddardagency.com

We acknowledge the financial support of the Canada Council for the Arts, the
Ontario Arts Council (OAC), the Ontario Media Development Corporation, and
the Government of Canada through the Canada Book Fund for our publishing
activities.

 Canada Council Conseil des arts
for the Arts du Canada

 ONTARIO ARTS COUNCIL
CONSEIL DES ARTS DE L'ONTARIO
an Ontario government agency
un organisme du gouvernement de l'Ontario

 Canada Ontario
Ontario Media Development
Corporation

Production Editor: MZK

LIBRARY AND ARCHIVES CANADA CATALOGUING IN PUBLICATION
Irani, Anosh, 1974-
   The Bombay plays : two plays : Bombay black & The matka king / Anosh Irani.

ISBN 978-0-88754-560-3

   I. Title. II. Title: Bombay black. III. Title: The matka king.

PS8617.R36B64 2007   C812'.6   C2007-900052-5

First edition: May 2007. Second printing: September 2014.
Printed and bound in Canada by Marquis Book Printing, Montreal

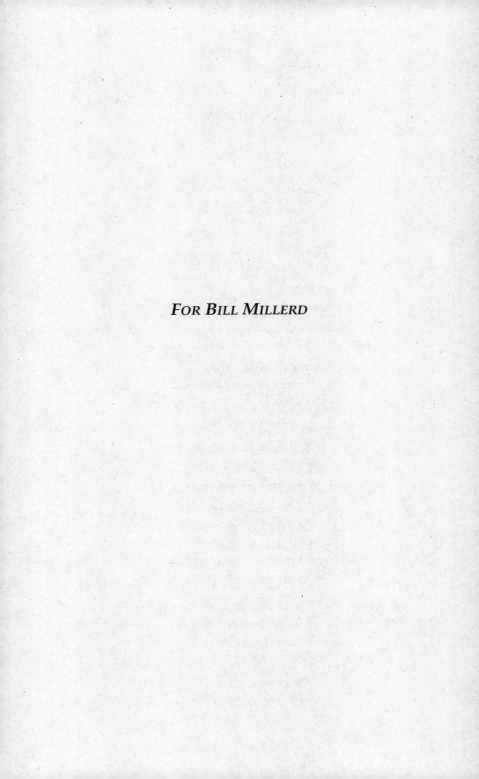

FOR BILL MILLERD

CONTENTS

INTRODUCTION

There is an unwritten rule, or, if it is writ, it lies
sculpted on God's arm. Once your journey begins,
you cannot end it. You can propel yourself off track,
skid in different mud, but it will only make your
journey that much longer.
                                    —*The Cripple and His Talismans*

Soft-spoken and quiet but not shy, Anosh Irani is one of many
newcomers to Canada who are laying claim to a special place in
their new country's artistic life.

Born in Bombay in 1974 and growing up in Byculla, in a Parsi
colony, Irani obtained his BComm (1995) from the University of
Bombay before embarking on a career as a copywriter in a Bombay
advertising agency. In 1998 he immigrated to Vancouver, where
distance from Bombay gave him perspective on the place of his
birth and upbringing. In Vancouver he studied Creative Writing
and Literature at Capilano College for one year, then transferred
to the Department of Creative Writing at the University of British
Columbia, where he obtained his BFA (2002) and MFA (2004) in
Creative Writing, a world he began to explore only after he had
reached Vancouver.

In *The Cripple and His Talismans* (2004), his much acclaimed
debut novel, Irani recounts the modern fable of an anonymous
hero who wanders through present-day Bombay in search of his
severed arm. Bombay is one of Irani's muses. Calling the city his
"favourite place in the world," Irani seeks to depict its multifaceted
culture. "It has a lot of soul," he reflects. "I will always consider it
home, but there's so much corruption, so much poverty. It's hard
for people to survive there." The journey through Bombay presents
the city's incredible suffering as well as its beautiful mysteries, the
novel being at once a magic-realist fable and a frank portrayal of
poverty and pain.

A master storyteller narrates the fable. "Ever since I was little, I
was good at telling stories, I was good at invention, making things
up on the spot," Irani says. "I come from a long line of storytellers,
none of whom are writers, but it's just that we used to get drunk

on family occasions and spread vicious lies about people who weren't there. That's the purest form of storytelling; you can't get any better than that."

In his second novel, the grimly realistic *The Song of Kahunsha* (2006), Chamdi, a young boy of ten, runs away from his Bombay orphanage, meeting up with Sumdi and Guddi, a brother and sister in a gang of beggars, and the trio wander the city in all its glory and gore. Sectarian violence in the form of bloody confrontations between Hindus and Muslims propels the plot forward to its tragic conclusion. Finding no evidence of love or compassion in the city, Chamdi seeks his own language, phrases that are spoken only in Kahunsha. "To him this means 'the city of no sadness.' Someday all sadness will die, he believes, and Bombay will be reborn as Kahunsha."

Irani, however, is not only a significant novelist. Even before the publication of his debut novel, his first play, *The Matka King*, premiered at the Vancouver Arts Club in October 2003. The protagonist is a eunuch who was castrated when he was ten years old. "Eunuchs are like stand-up comedians," comments Irani. "They're kind of scoundrels, but you like them because they're very funny. But at the same time they're vicious." Eunuchs live in a secretive Indian subculture, and *The Matka King* exposes some of this subculture in a tale of lust, love, and betrayal. Complete with its scenes of ghosts, human beings in cages, and death, the play transfixes its audience with its presentation of human beings caught in the tragedy of life.

In his second play, *Bombay Black*, which premiered at Toronto's Theatre Centre in January 2006, Irani reduces his cast to three people: the iron-willed Padma, her daughter Apsara, and a mysterious blind man, Kamal, whose visit sets in motion a harrowing tale of seduction, love, and revenge. At times beautifully lyrical, at other times realistically brutal, the play weaves into its plot elements of myth and magic that propel the characters (and the audience) into a fantastic flight of the imagination. At Toronto's Dora Mavor Moore Awards for 2006, the play won four Doras, including one for Irani for outstanding new play.

In the development of Canadian literature there is a curious phenomenon: many of our finest artists move easily from one genre to another. Leonard Cohen, for example, is a fine lyric poet who also writes impressive fiction. Margaret Atwood, Michael Ondaatje, and others, too, began their careers as poets, then moved on to become major fiction writers who have never forsaken their poetic art.

Irani moves effortlessly between two genres, fiction and drama, equally at ease in both. To his art he brings the welcome sounds and traditions of India, incorporating them into tales that are at once Indian and universal.

With this publication of Anosh Irani's first two plays, readers have the opportunity to savour his dramas and to admire their inventive complexities. Irani is a writer from whom we are going to hear much, much more.

David Staines

THE MATKA KING

l to r: Laara Sadiq as Chandni and Craig Veroni as Top Rani
photo by Andrée Lanthier

The Matka King premiered in October 2003 at the Arts Club Theatre, Vancouver, with the following company:

Craig Veroni	Top Rani
Marvin Ishmael	Guru Gantaal
Allan Zinyk	Satta
Laara Sadiq	Chandni
Anoushka Anderson Kirby	Aarti

Lois Anderson	Puppeteer
Bill Millerd	Artistic Managing Director
Rachel Ditor	Director & Dramaturg
Robert Gardiner	Set Design
Marsha Sibthorpe	Lighting Design
Barbara Clayden	Costume Design
Noah Drew	Sound Design
Chris Allan & Pamela Jakobs	Stage Managers
Anne Taylor	Assistant Stage Manager
Erin Harris	Design Assistant

The Matka King was workshopped and given public readings at the following play development events: ReACT: new plays in progress, 2002 & 2003 at the Arts Club Theatre, Vancouver, CrossCurrents Festival, 2002 & 2004 at the Factory Theatre, Toronto, and On the Verge, 2002 at the National Arts Centre, Ottawa. It was first published in *Canadian Theatre Review*.

CHARACTERS

TOP RANI   A eunuch in his thirties.

CHANDNI   A prostitute in her twenties.

AARTI   A ten-year-old girl.

SATTA   A gambler in his late thirties.

GANTAAL   A fortune teller of about fifty.

SETTING

The play takes place in Bombay at:
> a) Top Rani's brothel.
> b) Grant Road.

The time is the present.

ACT ONE

PROLOGUE

TOP RANI enters dressed in a sari. His hair is long but tied back. He has bangles on his wrists.

TOP RANI Come, come, enter my brothel. I have big-big girls for little-little prices. And little-little girls for big-big prices. Cheapest is ten rupees only. Surely you must have ten rupees. If you don't want complete insertion, then simple massage is also there. With happy ending. *(pause)* No? Oh, you enemy of love. You must be married. Is that your wife? Hello, beautiful. The word for tonight is "Legs." Spread the word. *(pause)* Let me show you around. You are in a red light district called Kamhathipura. There is a small merry-go-round just outside my window. It is operated by a pimp. Every evening, while his whores work, he gives their children free rides. Next to the merry-go-round is a doctor's dispensary. He has written the names of famous diseases on a white board—Syphilis, Gonorrhoea, and TB—none of which he can cure. Then there is Café Andaaz, where the prostitutes collect for their afternoon tea and pretend they are free. But in this city, no one is free. I realized that when I was ten years old. I was sent here by my father to work as a servant boy. I had dreams then. Now I can hardly remember what they were. The truth is there is no such thing as an Indian Dream. If there was, it died the day this city was born. Welcome to Bombay.

1.

Grant Road. December 30th. 8:45 p.m. Guru GANTAAL sits on the footpath. A large steel trunk rests in front of him. The sound of a car rushing past. Smoke from the car covers GANTAAL's face. He coughs violently.

GANTAAL Time for cigarette.

> *He removes a cigarette from behind his ear and puts it
> to his lips, but does not light it. The sound of another
> car going past. He cocks his head forward in antici-
> pation of the exhaust fumes. He exhales in time with the
> car's expulsion of smoke, pretending that he has blown
> cigarette smoke.*

Cars cause smoking. Smoking causes cigarettes. It is a vicious cycle.

> *Enter SATTA on a cycle. SATTA's cycle is old and
> beaten. It has a huge bugle-like horn on it and a large
> placard that says, "God is great but always late."*

A vicious cycle indeed.

SATTA Guru Gantaal. Please tell me. It's almost nine o'clock.

GANTAAL Okay. It's almost nine o'clock.

SATTA Don't do this to me. Tonight, I *have* to win. A lot of money is at stake.

> *SATTA shows him a fat wad of notes.*

GANTAAL Where did you get that?

SATTA I sold my kholi.

GANTAAL Sold it? Now where will you live?

SATTA There's no time to explain.

GANTAAL Then tonight I will show you something that is very precious to me.

> *SATTA rubs his hands in anticipation. GANTAAL
> opens the lid of the trunk and without looking in he puts
> his hand in. He screams in agony. He closes the lid and
> shakes his hand as though he has been stung.*

SATTA What happened?

GANTAAL My cobra bit me.

SATTA You have a cobra in there? Is it poisonous?

GANTAAL Very poisonous. I sometimes forget that the little one is still in there.

SATTA Shouldn't you be rushing to a hospital?

GANTAAL What for?

SATTA It bit you.

GANTAAL I used to be a snake charmer. Cobras never kill the hand that feeds them. He is just angry that he is locked in this trunk. But if *you* put your hand in, you will need to see a hospital. Anyway, I'm looking for my parrot.

SATTA A cobra and parrot stay in the same trunk?

GANTAAL The parrot is fake.

> *He brings SATTA closer to him. He opens the lid again.*

Satta, have you heard of any new methods?

SATTA I have heard of this new method called the Ant Race. It's very effective. You place ten sugar cubes in a row on the ground. Then you keep watch over the next few minutes as ants gather. Whichever cube the ants go to first, that is the opening number of the day. So if they go first to the cube placed fifth in the row, then the opening number is five. The cube the ants go to last, that is the closing number.

GANTAAL It works every time.

SATTA What works?

GANTAAL Your talk of opening and closing numbers is so boring that it has put my cobra to sleep.

SATTA Snakes can't hear. They're deaf.

GANTAAL You want the truth? It's not your talk that's putting it to sleep.

SATTA Good.

GANTAAL It's your body odour. Your smell is so bad the government will be forced to give you your own area code. Anyway, now I can safely remove the parrot from the trunk. Your smell has knocked out my cobra.

> *He removes a parrot from the trunk and places it on the lid.*

Where is your pack of cards?

> *SATTA removes a pack of cards from his shirt pocket.*

Why a new pack everyday? You must have spent a fortune only on buying cards.

SATTA I have heard that *he* uses a new pack everyday. So I must also use a new pack otherwise we will never be able to predict the numbers.

GANTAAL It.

SATTA It?

GANTAAL Not *him*. It. A eunuch is an "It." That is why the name Top Rani. The Head Queen.

SATTA He is also called "The Matka King." In which case, he is a he.

GANTAAL Fine. Let us refer to the eunuch as a he. Now place numbers one to ten in a row.

> *SATTA places the ten cards on the lid of the trunk.*

The parrot will choose one number with its beak. That will be tonight's opening number.

SATTA But the parrot is fake.

GANTAAL I am aware of that.

SATTA Then how will it choose the number?

GANTAAL Watch.

> *They both stare at the parrot. GANTAAL makes absurd parrot sounds. The parrot, of course, remains stationary.*

It's taking its time.

SATTA What are you talking about? It's stationary.

> *GANTAAL grabs the parrot by the neck and bangs it down on the card placed second in the row.*

GANTAAL Number two. Opening on two. The bird has spoken.

SATTA You banged it face down on the trunk!

GANTAAL Are you doubting my powers?

SATTA Yes!

GANTAAL Good. Doubt gets rid of certainty.

SATTA What?

GANTAAL Bet on two. It's almost nine o'clock.

> *SATTA shakes his head, mounts his cycle and leaves.*
> *GANTAAL places the parrot back in the trunk. The*
> *cobra bites again.*

(to cobra) Again you have woken up. This time you will be in a deep sleep. The only cobra I know who falls asleep to bad smell: the natural odour of this city.

> *He keeps the lid of the trunk wide open.*

(to sewer in distance) Beautiful sewer! As natural as a gurgling brook… *(to cobra)* Ah, you're getting drowsy… *(to breeze)* Oh wafting breeze from the public bathroom, please come in, come in… who needs the scent of jasmine when…

> *He looks down in disgust. GANTAAL lifts his foot up*
> *and examines his sole. He has just stepped in something.*
> *He scrapes it off his foot into the trunk.*

(delightfully to cobra) Knockout. It works every time.

> *He slams the lid shut.*

2.

> *The brothel. December 30th. 8:55 p.m. TOP RANI is*
> *seated on a swing that is suspended from the ceiling by*
> *long iron rods.*

TOP RANI Matka is a very simple game, okay? At nine o' clock each night, I pick one card. I call that the opening number. At midnight, I pick one more. The closing number. I post each number outside. Within minutes the people of this city will gather to check if they have been able to guess correctly. The tea stall owner will tell the man on the cycle. The man on the cycle will stop at all the traffic signals and tell the taxiwalas, the taxiwalas will tell their passengers who will go home and tell their household. All those who have placed bets with their bookies will calculate—up or down? If they guessed the number correctly and bet their weekly pay on it, they will have an extra round of drinks. If they guessed wrong and bet their weekly pay on it... they might hang themselves from a ceiling fan. *(pause)* But gambling is not about money. Only amateurs think that. Gambling is about good health. It makes your blood circulate better, you sleep less and are alert, and your heart does not waste its time on love because it is too busy beating out of anticipation.

> *Enter CHANDNI. She carries a silver tray in her hands. In it is a stainless steel container that holds a red mixture.*

CHANDNI   It's almost nine o'clock.

TOP RANI   Has the matka been washed?

CHANDNI   Yes, Top Rani.

TOP RANI   Is the red mixture ready?

> *She places the steel container in front of him. She then dips her finger in the red mixture.*

CHANDNI   It looks like blood. What's it for?

TOP RANI   *(indicating her red finger)* If you put your finger in my business you *will* get cut.

> *She turns to leave.*

Those flowers in your hair. Are they fresh?

CHANDNI   Yes, Top Rani.

TOP RANI   Are all the daughters ready for the night?

CHANDNI   Except Sudha. She's sick.

TOP RANI She's falling sick too often. I can't afford to keep her if this continues.

CHANDNI But she's worked here for many years. She must be looked after.

TOP RANI This is not a government job.

CHANDNI What happens if *I* fall ill?

TOP RANI I will be plunged into darkness. You are the red light of my life.

> *CHANDNI turns around to leave.*

Chandni.

CHANDNI What.

TOP RANI Make Sudha drink lots of water. Water can cure any sickness.

CHANDNI Then maybe *I* should drink water. To prevent my legs from spreading.

TOP RANI Ah, Chandni… when I brought you here, you were so young and quiet. But look at you now!

CHANDNI Thanks to your fine parenting.

TOP RANI Don't thank me, thank God. It is *in* God's will. When God left this earth, he left a will. In it, he declared that you and six other girls, now your sisters, were to be placed under my care. That is why I say it is *in* his will. By operating this brothel, I'm merely honouring God's wishes.

CHANDNI Unfortunately, I'm not.

TOP RANI Why is that?

CHANDNI God wants me to take these nails and pierce your eyes.

TOP RANI Must be a different God.

> *He tells her to leave. She exits.*

It's nine o' clock. Time for the opening number.

TOP RANI walks to a small wooden cupboard. He opens the cupboard and removes a pack of cards and a blindfold. He walks to the matka, stands above it, and opens the seal around the pack. He separates the coloured cards from the pack and shows them to the audience.

Jacks, Queens, Kings, and Jokers. They are, by nature, separate from the pack.

He throws them to the floor.

Royalty and commoners do not mix. *(pause)* Before I pull the opening number, I always do something to honour those who have lost their lives to gambling. I call it my auspicious invocation. It is extremely holy.

He spits into the matka.

There. I've paid my respects.

He empties the cards into the matka and blindfolds himself. Then he reaches into the matka and pulls out one card. He takes off his blindfold, inspects the card, and shows it to the audience.

Ten is the opening number. Time to disclose it to the public. It's the ten of diamonds. It means I'm going to find a jewel soon.

3.

Grant Road. December 30th. Ten minutes later. Enter SATTA on his cycle. GANTAAL has fallen asleep. SATTA seems angry.

SATTA Wake up!

He blows the cycle horn.

Wake up you...!

GANTAAL gets up with a jerk.

GANTAAL Ten! Ten is the opening number!

SATTA   I know that, you fool.

GANTAAL   My dreams are very lucid.

SATTA   Your lucid dreams are of no use if you get the number *after* it is pulled. Where is your parrot?

GANTAAL   Why?

SATTA   I want to kill it! I lost a lot of money.

GANTAAL   So no more gambling for you?

SATTA   I'm betting on tonight's closing number.

GANTAAL   What?

SATTA   It's the last bet of the year.

GANTAAL   Last bet? But today is the 30th.

SATTA   Last *Matka* bet of the year. Tomorrow night no Matka. On the 31st, Top Rani plays "Raja Kheench."

GANTAAL   Ah, "Pull the King." The game that nobody has ever won.

SATTA   I know. That eunuch must be cheating. That is why *tonight* will be the biggest bet of my life. Seven thousand rupees.

GANTAAL   Seven thousand!

SATTA   It's all I have left from the sale of my kholi. I have a dead tip. Dead accurate. It's for tonight's closing number. The tip comes straight from the hand that washes the matka. Her name is Chandni. She's a worker at Top Rani's.

GANTAAL   Worker. Why don't you use the correct word?

SATTA   Because I have a daughter too. It's a shame, a shame.

GANTAAL   But it's not a shame to use her.

SATTA   I'm not using her. This jeweller whose shop is at Grant Road goes to Chandni very often for his...

GANTAAL   Oiling?

SATTA Oiling-boiling. So Chandni revealed to him that for the last bet of the year, Top Rani does not pull the closing number from the matka. He simply bases closing number according to a whim.

GANTAAL I'm afraid to ask what the whim of a eunuch can be.

SATTA Which daughter earns the most money. This year it has been Chandni. She is the first daughter. So the closing number is one.

GANTAAL Who told you this?

SATTA My sister-in-law. She sweeps the jeweller's shop. She heard the jeweller discuss this over the phone. That is why I say it is a dead tip. There's no room for mistakes. And I'm not going to place the bet with any bookie-fookie. I'm going straight to the top.

GANTAAL Top Rani.

SATTA He gives terrific odds. My plan is foolproof.

GANTAAL It is the proof of a fool. I am not betting no matter how dead the tip.

SATTA That's not why I'm here. I want you to look after my daughter while I go and place my bet. I've already made an appointment with Top Rani.

GANTAAL I am Guru Gantaal! World-renowned fortune teller! I will not look after your daughter! Let your *wife* do it.

SATTA My wife is dead. I've told you many times.

GANTAAL Where is your daughter?

SATTA She's just round the corner drinking a lassi.

>   *SATTA whistles loudly to call her. Enter AARTI.*

GANTAAL *(to AARTI)* What is your name?

>   *AARTI does not respond. She looks shyly at SATTA.*

Don't be shy. Tell me your name.

SATTA Her name is Aarti.

GANTAAL Did I ask you?

SATTA Aarti cannot speak. Ever since her mother died…

GANTAAL I… I'm sorry.

SATTA Aarti, I have to go for some time. You stay here and… stare at this silly old man.

> *AARTI holds on to SATTA to prevent him from leaving.*

I have to go.

> *SATTA exits on the cycle. AARTI stares at GANTAAL.*

GANTAAL Of course I'm silly. I'm a real silly man. You are an angel. You don't *need* to speak. Look at your wings. You have such beautiful moon coloured wings.

> *AARTI is not impressed. GANTAAL pretends he hears something.*

Can you hear that Aarti?

> *She shakes her head—no.*

The whispering. That is Aroramanyu. The Warrior Angel. He wants to tell you what moon colour is.

> *He pretends to repeat Aroramanyu's words.*

Thousands of years ago, the earth was a happy and pure place. Slowly slowly it became bad. First the sins were very small—the worst thing people would do was lie. But then the sins increased. People started robbing, stealing, and beating each other up. Then murder started happening. God got very upset. He got up from his big chair near the sun and put his hand out and grabbed all the bad people in his fist. They were all shouting and screaming and choking… and God took them, made this round ball, and put them all in that. That is your moon. But then—all these bad people tried to escape from the moon. So God called his biggest and most powerful angel—Aroramanyu! And to prevent the moon prisoners from escaping, God tore off Aroramanyu's wing.

> *AARTI does not like this.*

He covered the moon with this wing so the prisoners could not escape. When they realized they were trapped, they began to cry and their tears stained this wing. The white wing became a different, translucent colour. That is your moon colour! *(pause)* But do you know *why* he is telling you this?

She shakes her head—no.

He is saying that his other wing is for *your* protection. He will send it to you, but only if you ask for it. You can do it. Through your thoughts. Thoughts are more powerful than words. They can travel a longer distance. *(pause)* Open your mouth. Catch your thoughts in your fist.

She grabs unspoken words from her mouth.

And throw them to the moon! Keep looking up.

GANTAAL pulls out a white bedsheet from the trunk and covers AARTI with it. The sheet is old and worn.

He is saying that *this* is other wing. It will always cover you and protect you from harm.

He listens to Aroramanyu again.

What? Oh. Aarti, I have some bad news for you. Aroramanyu says he cannot protect your father. You know why? Because your father is *so* boring, *so* boring. All he talks about is opening number and closing number and opening number and closing number... one of these days I will set my cobra loose on that idiot.

The sound of a car in the distance.

Quick, cover your head. *(covering AARTI's head with the sheet)* Smoking is bad for you.

GANTAAL takes the cigarette from behind his ear and puts it to his lips. He sucks in. The car passes by but no exhaust fumes.

No exhaust. Must be a foreign car.

4.

The brothel. Ten minutes later. TOP RANI is seated on the swing. But he is unseen. CHANDNI leans out of a window and is selling herself. She is talking to SATTA who is on the street.

CHANDNI Kya darling? Ready for action?

SATTA No… I'm here for…

CHANDNI Don't be shy. I will make your Monday a Sunday.

SATTA But today is Sunday.

CHANDNI Kya darling, it's only an expression. You want deluxe package or ordinary? In deluxe I make sounds also.

She moans in complete boredom.

SATTA No, you don't understand. I'm not here for that. No one must see me talking to you.

CHANDNI Okay. Fry your own onions.

SATTA I did not mean it like that.

CHANDNI Then how you meant?

SATTA I'm here to see Top Rani. I have an appointment.

CHANDNI Come up. I will open for you.

She opens the door for him.

That's all I ever do. Open.

Enter SATTA who tries to adjust to the darkness of the brothel. TOP RANI is still on the swing, unseen.

You must be Satta then.

SATTA Don't tell anyone.

CHANDNI Man or mosquito?

SATTA It will look bad if…

CHANDNI If someone sees you with me? What do you expect here, your mother's arms?

SATTA I just want to meet Top Rani. Please.

TOP RANI You will.

He is now visible. CHANDNI leaves.

SATTA I want to...

TOP RANI I know what you want. If it is not a special night with one of my daughters, it is money.

SATTA I do not need anything. I have come to place a bet.

TOP RANI What bet?

SATTA For tonight's closing number.

TOP RANI Go to a bookie. I do not take bets.

SATTA I've heard you give better odds.

TOP RANI How much are you willing to place?

SATTA Seven thousand.

TOP RANI Seven thousand. You do not look like you can afford that sum. You must know something I don't.

SATTA I need to win the money for my brother's operation. He has a hole in his heart.

TOP RANI And I have one from where I shit. Do not waste my time.

SATTA I am in heavy debt. Do you know Khalil Bhai?

TOP RANI You owe that gangster money?

SATTA Fifty thousand. If I do not pay him...

TOP RANI He will kill you.

SATTA nods.

I do not accept small bets. If you will increase the amount, I will consider.

SATTA I'm not begging for money. I'm just asking that you accept my bet. Give me the odds that will allow me to repay Khalil Bhai.

TOP RANI Why are you so sure you will win? Something is black in the gravy.

SATTA I have to pay Khalil Bhai by tomorrow morning.

TOP RANI Then it is rude of me not to grant a dying man his last wish. But the problem still is that the bet is not enough. You will have to raise the stakes.

SATTA But I have nothing. Absolutely nothing. I promise. I've even sold my house.

TOP RANI You have nothing. That is not what I have heard.

SATTA I can assure you that whatever you have heard is wrong.

TOP RANI Then it is wrong to say that you have a daughter? Chandni!

Enter CHANDNI.

(to SATTA) What happened? Suddenly you are silent? Just like your daughter. *(to CHANDNI)* What is his daughter's name?

CHANDNI Aarti.

TOP RANI Age.

CHANDNI Ten.

TOP RANI Colour of hair.

CHANDNI Dark brown.

TOP RANI Eyes.

CHANDNI Black.

TOP RANI Favourite hero.

CHANDNI Shahrukh Khan.

TOP RANI Best movie.

CHANDNI "Dil To Pagal Hai."

TOP RANI Mother.

CHANDNI Killed. In riots.

TOP RANI *(to SATTA)* You shake like a leaf. Chandni must be correct. I will accept your bet. If you lose, I get the seven thousand. *Plus* your daughter. She will be well looked after. She will earn more than you do. I know what you are thinking: my daughter will never be a whore. *(pointing to CHANDNI)* I'm sure her father thought the same before he drank himself to death. It's what men do. They abandon. And we eunuchs are the ones that are ridiculed.

SATTA That is impossible. I will never allow it.

TOP RANI Then it is impossible for me to take your bet. Goodbye.

> *SATTA turns and walks hastily to the exit.*

Fifty to one odds.

> *SATTA stops, but his back is still to TOP RANI.*

Fifty to one. Three and a half lakhs on a bet of seven thousand. Not only can you repay Khalil Bhai but you can also buy your kholi back. And more.

> *SATTA faces TOP RANI.*

But I agree. A daughter is too much to ask.

> *SATTA walks up to TOP RANI and hands him an envelope that contains the money and a slip of paper with the number he is betting on.*

SATTA I accept your condition.

TOP RANI Some people take more time to buy vegetables. *(pause)* If you win, your money will be ready. If not, I will make sure Aarti is here first thing tomorrow morning. It is good. Tomorrow is the last day of the year. Men pay a lot on New Year's Eve.

*SATTA exits. TOP RANI gives the envelope to
CHANDNI. She exits.*

Let me tell you a story. Don't worry, everybody loves stories.
(pause) Twenty-five years ago, there lived a man named
Surya—handsome as the sun itself. Women looked beautiful
in his light, baby moons reflecting his own beauty. When
they made love to their husbands they cried out *his* name
until their throats dried up. The first time I saw Surya, he
was tied to a tree, shivering with fear. It was nine o'clock
on New Year's Eve and I was ten years old, a servant boy
carrying a matka on my head… *(He points to the earthen pot.)*
this very matka, to fetch water from a nearby well. Surya
had raped one of the men's wives. He would be set on fire
for it. Men gathered round the tree and started to take off
his clothes to shame him as he had shamed the woman.
Once Surya was naked, his innocence was obvious. He was a
eunuch. *(pause)* But the men were not satisfied: "If our wives
burn for him, he shall burn too." They poured gasoline over
him, lit a match, and fled. I ran to the well, filled this matka
with water, and tried to douse the flames. I poured water
into his mouth. He drank a little, then touched this matka
and blessed it. He said: "A king will make you whole." That
same day, at the stroke of midnight, *I* became a eunuch.

TOP RANI spots CHANDNI walking towards the door.

Where do you think you're going?

CHANDNI   To a movie.

TOP RANI   What for?

CHANDNI   To watch it.

TOP RANI   You can't go.

CHANDNI   Why not?

TOP RANI   I don't feel well.

CHANDNI   Maybe you have what Sudha has.

TOP RANI   Why? Is she dying?

CHANDNI   She looks like a skeleton.

TOP RANI   Good. The same showpiece over and over is stale.

CHANDNI   Then let me go from this place. I am your oldest prostitute.

TOP RANI   You be grateful that I have given you the chance to put food in your mouth.

CHANDNI   That's not the only thing you've helped me put in my mouth.

TOP RANI   I rescued you from a gutter. Your own father did not think you were worth it.

CHANDNI   I am not worthless. *You* are. I'm going for that movie. The men in the movies have something you don't. Something you never will.

> *TOP RANI walks to the corner and picks out a cricket bat. He circles around CHANDNI and makes sure that she notices the bat.*

TOP RANI   Do you know what I wanted to become when I was a boy? A cricketer! A century on my debut in England! I'd look dashing in my spotless white uniform. After the match, the British girls would rush to me and say, "I say, old chap, mister brown boy, can we stroke your bat?" But since I'm from India, I'd feel shy. We are a backward country, we are not used to advances. Then the girls would say, "We have heard your bat is finer than English willow. Would you like to rest it on our pillow?"

> *He grazes the bat along CHANDNI's thighs.*

One day you're a young boy playing cricket staring at the sun…

> *The sun shines very brightly on him. The way he holds the bat suggests he is about to hit CHANDNI.*

The next day…

> *Blackout.*

5.

Grant Road. Ten minutes later. AARTI is seated on top of GANTAAL's trunk. She still has the sheet draped over her and seems happy. Enter SATTA. He is very anxious.

SATTA Where is that fool? I can't believe he left you alone. *(to himself)* I can't believe what I have done. How did this happen?

He goes to AARTI. He holds her.

Aarti, I will never abandon you. Do you understand? No matter what happens. Remember what your mother used to say—be brave. When times are tough, be brave. If you are afraid, you will lose. If you are brave, you will win.

She wipes the sweat off his brow. He puts his head in her lap. She caresses his face.

Don't worry. Your papa is okay. Your papa is okay. *(looking skywards)* I just wish that your mother would give me a sign that everything will be okay. Please, Shanti. Please...

He paces about restlessly. A dog barks once. SATTA freezes. He listens.

Did you hear that Aarti? How many times did the dog bark?

AARTI holds up one finger.

Once! Just once! A dog *never* barks once. Dogs always bark twice, or three times. Don't you see what this means? I bet on one. The closing number is *one*. I am right. That dog barked *once*. *(pause)* Oh God, what if it barks again? Don't bark again. Please. Maybe I should find it and kill it. Then it won't bark anymore.

He rushes in the direction of the bark. GANTAAL enters.

GANTAAL Where are you going?

SATTA To kill a dog.

GANTAAL What?

SATTA It must not bark again!

> *GANTAAL holds SATTA who is near hysterical. He
> looks at AARTI who seems afraid. He takes out some
> coins from his pocket and gives them to AARTI.*

GANTAAL Angel, it is lassi-time!

> *She takes the money and exits.*

What is wrong with you? You're scaring the girl.

SATTA I did it. I can't believe I did it.

GANTAAL Did what?

SATTA I placed my bet. This is a question of my life.

GANTAAL The question of your life is whether you can trust
your wife's sister. *She* has given you the tip.

SATTA I trust her with my life.

GANTAAL Seven thousand rupees is a lot of money. If you
lose, you have nothing. Who will look after your daughter
then?

SATTA Top Rani.

GANTAAL Satta, that is something even I would not joke about.

SATTA I'm serious. I owe a lot of money—fifty thousand—to
Khalil Bhai.

GANTAAL Fifty thousand! When did this happen? I thought
you played small.

SATTA My gambling increased after my wife died. If alcohol
makes you remember, gambling makes you forget. I
have failed in my duty towards Aarti. I have failed. I'm a
miserable father.

GANTAAL You are a bad gambler, but a good father.

SATTA I've wagered Aarti in a Matka bet with Top Rani.

GANTAAL What?

SATTA I've wagered Aarti in a Matka bet with Top Rani.

GANTAAL What do you mean?

SATTA I've wagered Aarti in a Matka bet with Top Rani.

GANTAAL Will you stop repeating? I heard you.

SATTA I am saying it over and over so that it sinks into my wretched skull!

GANTAAL I cannot believe it.

SATTA If I do not repay Khalil Bhai by tomorrow morning, I am a dead man. Who will care for her then? I'm glad her mother is not alive to see this.

GANTAAL Why didn't you just place the seven thousand?

SATTA Top Rani refused to accept the seven thousand. The dead tip will not fail me. I know it. The dead tip will not fail me.

GANTAAL Satta, I don't know what to say.

SATTA Just tell me I will win!

GANTAAL Call the whole thing off.

SATTA My days are numbered. Khalil Bhai has given me a final warning. If I do not pay him by tomorrow, I am a dead man.

GANTAAL There must be another way out.

SATTA Like what? Maybe we should ask your parrot.

GANTAAL Even he will be speechless in this matter. *(pause)* But I overheard a conversation last night between the parrot and the cobra. Do you want to know what the parrot said?

SATTA No.

GANTAAL Good. The parrot said that when he was alive, his name was Polly. He was owned by a fortune teller. Now Polly was a very gifted parrot because he could tell the Matka numbers nine times out of ten. Lots of people came to Polly. "Polly the Punter, Polly the Punter, can you tell us the Matka number?" Then Polly would say the number out loud. The gamblers of this city respected Polly so much they

started calling *him* "The Matka King." *Until one day. Saala,*
there is always *until one day* in everything. When you buy
mangos, they taste good *until one day* they taste bad. You
wear a pant that you like every day *until one day* you are too
fat to wear it. A person is alive *until one day* the person is
dead. *(pause)* Where was I?

SATTA Polly the Punter...

GANTAAL So Polly the Punter and his master were really
happy *until one day*... people came to kidnap Polly. They
held Polly by the neck so he could not scream for help.
They squeezed his voice box too hard. All the magic was in
Polly's voice box. So Polly turned to stone. Right there in the
kidnapper's hands. That is what Polly the Punter told the
cobra.

SATTA Why didn't someone squeeze my voice box? I would
not have agreed to Top Rani's wager.

GANTAAL All will be well. Trust in God.

SATTA God is great but always late.

GANTAAL Ssh!

SATTA I don't care if he hears me. Where was God when my
wife died? Hah? Which garden was he tending when those
rioting bastards killed her? They were stoning the mill owner
who was running for his life. And what happened? They hit
my Shanti. I'm ready to accept whatever fate comes my way.
You can tell God that.

GANTAAL I will. But there is one problem.

SATTA What.

GANTAAL God does not come to this city anymore. Poor
fellow cannot bear the smell.

> *SATTA smiles.*

It is a good omen that you are smiling. No harm will come
over your daughter. But I think after tonight's closing
number, you will never play Matka again.

SATTA nods.

Now you are relaxed and I am nervous.

> *He removes a cigarette from behind his ear, and looks to the end of the road.*

Where is a car when you need one?

6.

> *The brothel. December 30th. Almost midnight. It is dark. Oil lamps have been randomly placed and lit. It gives the brothel an eerie look.*

TOP RANI I thought if I waited, the king that Surya spoke of would seek me. Throughout history, kings and eunuchs have shared a special relationship. At times of war, eunuchs served as protectors of the kings' harems. For eunuchs were strong enough to keep the women safe, yet unable to make love to them. So in the past, *kings* have needed eunuchs. It was the people of this city who led that king to me… when they bestowed upon me the title of "The Matka King." I realized it was *me* Surya was talking about. I had to make *myself* whole. So to honour Surya's death, I do not pick an opening number on New Year's Eve. And at the stroke of midnight, this city plays a special game. Raja Kheench: Pull the King. I throw Jacks, Queens, Kings, and Jokers into the matka along with the rest of the cards. It's the one time I want gamblers all across the city to win. For I know that if I pull a king…

> *He picks up a dark grey, cylindrical piece of stone, shaped like a phallus, in his hands. It is wide at the base, but tapers at the top.*

…I will be a man again. You see this thing?

> *He holds the phallus like an offering.*

It is used to grind masalas. You place a thick slab of stone on the ground. You put the masala on that slab and sit on your haunches. You grind the masala to a paste. It is hard work—

you rock back and forth, back and forth, and your limbs ache from squatting. But you do it because you are a servant boy and it is what you are meant to do. But that does not mean you cannot think of other things while you are doing it: of cricket and how you run away when you break someone else's windowpane. That is what gives the masala its flavour—the thoughts of the person at the time of grinding. If you think about dead people, the masala will taste stale. If you are homesick for your village, the masala will taste bittersweet. And your master cannot understand how the masala tastes different every time because the ingredients never change. *(indicating the phallus)* But this is now a part of me. It's almost midnight. Odd time to be doing all this natak. Odd time, no? *(blowing out lamp nearest to him)* Odd time to be woken from your sleep to see eyes shining in the dark. *(blowing out second lamp)* Odd time for you to be dragged by people you don't know into your master's kitchen. *(blowing out third lamp)* Odd time for you to hear them say, "You will no longer be a man." *(blowing last lamp out to a blackout)* My hands are tied; my mouth is gagged. I cannot see their faces because it is dark. But I can see eyes.

> *Parts of the kitchen start glowing. At great speed, the oil lamps come on again.*

They all have long hair and wear saris. They hold oil lamps in their palms and circle round and round like an offering. They remove my shirt. As they take my shirt, the bangles on their wrist...

> *The sound of bangles clinking rapidly.*

Then they sit on my chest so I cannot move. I see their dark faces. They have colour on their lips all red-red. In the centre of the forehead, a bindi. They tear my short pants. They turn me around. And put this delightful object inside me. I pass out from the pain of this... *(indicates sodomy)* so I do not feel the pain of... *(indicates castration)* When I open my eyes again it is midnight. They all shout, "You are pure, you are cured." Where there should be the mark of a man, there is mud. To heal the wound, to stop the bleeding. They put mud. Mud behind also. To heal the wound, to stop the bleeding. Mud,

like trees grow from. They take the man from me and give
me mud in return. Mud.

> *He dips the phallus in the red mixture that CHANDNI*
> *had placed in the tray. The phallus now looks*
> *blood-smeared. He places it upright on the swing.*

By midnight tomorrow, I must be *worthy* of being whole
again. Otherwise I will not pull a king. So I re-live the worst
moment of my life to purify myself for the best. It is called
the Myth of Merit.

> *He lifts his sari just a little, faces audience, and slowly*
> *sits onto the phallus. He is in tremendous pain.*
> *Simultaneously, there is the sound of thunder. It starts*
> *to rain heavily. He stays there for a moment, regains his*
> *composure. He still breathes in and out slowly as the*
> *phallus is in him.*

It is midnight... the last Matka bet of the year.

> *The matka lies at the foot of the swing. So do the*
> *blindfold and pack of cards. He uses his feet to bring the*
> *matka directly in front of him. He points to the night*
> *sky.*

It never rains this time of the year. It means the night sky is
weeping. It could be for any one of us, for the sky looks over
us all.

> *He separates coloured cards from the pack, empties the*
> *rest of the cards into the matka, and blindfolds himself.*
> *Then he puts his hand in the matka and pulls the closing*
> *number. He removes his blindfold and stares straight at*
> *the audience. He smiles.*

7.

> *Grant Road. Fifteen minutes later. Guru GANTAAL*
> *is absent but his trunk is on the street. We hear music.*
> *Street performers playing the drums, celebrating. Enter*
> *SATTA. He looks absolutely dejected. He is drenched in*
> *the rain. A few moments later, AARTI enters. The white*

> *sheet still covers her. The sheet is wet. She goes over*
> *to him, tugs his shirt, and starts clapping her hands to*
> *cheer him up.*

SATTA Yes, dance, my angel. Dance! It will soon be the New
Year! A new beginning for all of us! *(looking skywards)*
Look—all the stars are out. Stars are the eyes of all the
people who have left this earth. They are watching over us.
Look—those are your mother's eyes. I know… because I am
unable to look into them.

> *Enter GANTAAL.*

GANTAAL Angel! I'm so relieved to see you!

> *GANTAAL covers her head with the bedsheet and wipes*
> *her dry. While doing so, he talks to SATTA.*

I take it all clear? Jackpot?

SATTA Yes, baba. All clear. Not to fear.

GANTAAL So where are you going now? To pay Khalil Bhai?

SATTA Later, later.

GANTAAL What do you mean later? You don't keep Khalil
Bhai waiting.

SATTA But we are celebrating.

> *The sound of thunder.*

Even the sky is celebrating! It's okay. Everything is okay.
Listen to me.

> *GANTAAL stares at SATTA for a moment. The three*
> *of them listen to the sound of thunder. There is also the*
> *sound of a convoy of cars approaching.*

GANTAAL Listen to all those cars…

> *The cars get louder.*

Never in my life have I seen so many cars on this road. How
much commotion! As if anybody cares? Does Aarti care?
Does Satta care?

*SATTA nervously shakes his head, somewhat distracted.
He looks at the cars in the distance, but his mind is
clearly somewhere else. The sound gets louder.*

This is my home! Don't come and blow smoke in my face
and remind me that I am poor! How will you like it if I come
to your home and shit? Hah?

*The cars are very near and are moving at great speed.
SATTA looks very disturbed and nervous. He looks
skywards. Suddenly, everything goes quiet. Lights only
on SATTA.*

SATTA   Aarti, your mother is calling us… we must go to your
mother…

*The sound of the cars is heard once again. SATTA yanks
AARTI by the hand and jumps into oncoming traffic.
The glare of headlights on SATTA and AARTI as the
cars are only a foot away.*

GANTAAL   Aarti!

There is a sickening thud and crash of cars.

END OF ACT ONE

ACT TWO

1.

The brothel. December 31st. Sunrise. TOP RANI reclines on his swing.

TOP RANI If you think about it, from the time we are born, we are all prostitutes. From the time we are born. What is the first thing a child learns? To suck. You come from a hole and then you start sucking. It's the skill you acquire first on this earth. So why stop utilizing it? Why is Chandni so good at her work? She never stopped sucking. Prostitution is what we are meant to do. All these other things: doctors, lawyers, accountants, these are inventions that deviate us from our true destiny.

Enter CHANDNI. She has just woken up. She walks with her legs slightly apart.

CHANDNI I'm so sore.

TOP RANI It's a good sign you still get sore. Men don't want the well too deep.

CHANDNI No one's forcing them to fetch water. *(pause)* Why are you smiling?

TOP RANI Today is a special day.

CHANDNI I forgot. "Raja Kheench." You'll make lots of money.

TOP RANI "Pull the King" isn't about money.

CHANDNI What if you *do* pull a king? You will lose everything you own when people come to collect their winnings.

TOP RANI By that time, I will not care about money. I will not care…

CHANDNI Why do you always act so strange just before the New Year?

TOP RANI Aah, Chandni, Chandni. You have come a long way. We have come a long way. Come. Talk to me.

CHANDNI   I have work to do. Otherwise you will remind me that you picked me up from the gutter.

TOP RANI   Not today. Today, I just want my daughter next to me. Come. Press my feet. You'll feel better.

> *CHANDNI sits on the floor with his feet in her lap.*

You're a very lucky girl.

CHANDNI   Yes, I've been saved from the gutter.

> *CHANDNI starts pressing his feet too hard.*

TOP RANI   With some love. What are feet if they are not pressed with love?

CHANDNI   I cannot make out whether you are happy or sad.

TOP RANI   And people cannot make out if I am man or woman. It is sad that a hijra is made by what he doesn't have. I have to show people what they can't see. That is why you are lucky. You can show your breasts because you have them and it is what people want. But people are repelled by what I don't have. Chandni, you are one country. You take off all your clothes and tell me: "Look, look, I have this terrible nuclear bomb. It will destroy you." And I am the country that laughs in your face. I simply lift my sari: "Look, look, I have this terrible nothing." And of the two countries, *you* will surrender.

CHANDNI   I surrendered a long time ago. *(pause)* Will I ever be free?

TOP RANI   You can't be free. You have to charge.

CHANDNI   Will I ever be able to say no if I don't want to press your feet?

TOP RANI   No.

CHANDNI   Even though I'm your first daughter?

TOP RANI   That's why I hold you so close. You're my number one prostitute.

CHANDNI   I'm proud, so proud.

TOP RANI You have my blessing.

CHANDNI I don't want your blessing.

TOP RANI (*holding her chin in his hand*) Then what do you want, Chandni? You have everything. You have nice breasts, a home, a family. You have *me*. Don't you love me?

CHANDNI With all my heart.

TOP RANI Sometimes a heart can be the wrong colour. What is the colour of your heart, Chandni?

CHANDNI The colour of your sari.

TOP RANI Purple?

CHANDNI My heart is bruised.

TOP RANI I love colours. They're so… colourful.

CHANDNI Can I wear your sari?

TOP RANI Of course. But you will never leave here with it.

CHANDNI Then I don't want it.

TOP RANI Now don't sit there with a black face.

CHANDNI If my future is black, my face will be the same colour.

TOP RANI And the future is shaped by betrayal.

CHANDNI What do you mean?

TOP RANI Trees, fire, mud, and…

> *TOP RANI reaches for a small switch that is connected to a lightbulb. He puts it on. Below the lightbulb is a small cage. In it is a little girl with her head in her knees. It is AARTI.*

…betrayal. The four constants of this world. Betrayal is a part of nature. We are all betrayed at some point in our lives. You were betrayed by your father who drank himself to death. In turn, you will betray too.

CHANDNI I have no intention of doing so.

TOP RANI Can you understand why her father gambled her away?

CHANDNI No.

TOP RANI Trees, fire, mud, and *betrayal*. Now. Meet your new student.

CHANDNI I will teach her nothing.

TOP RANI Why not?

CHANDNI She's only ten.

TOP RANI So she will earn ten times more. *(to AARTI)* You will charge more than Chandni. Indian men believe that if they take a virgin, they will be cured of all disease. Do you know how precious you are? *(pause)* Why are you silent?

CHANDNI She doesn't speak.

TOP RANI I forgot. Then how will she make sounds? Men love sounds. *(pause)* What if I record you and play it in the background when she is working? *(to AARTI)* Is dubbing okay with you?

> We hear a phone ring. It is TOP RANI's cell phone. He answers it.

Top Rani and Company. *(pause)* Hah, jeweller *bhai*…

> There is a pause while he listens to the jeweller's words. He snaps his fingers and sends CHANDNI away.

Which bookie are you talking about? Give me a name and I will give you his testicles. You can't just tell me that a bookie told you Matka is fixed. Tell me, how long ago did I start Matka? Ten years. Not one illegal incident. There's no cheating going on. Now give me the name of the bookie that said this. Why are you not revealing the name? I think *you* are unhappy about something…

> The jeweller hangs up on him.

A bookie would not dare make this accusation. Our jeweller friend is unhappy. I will have to research why.

He puts the phone down. Enter CHANDNI. She looks shaken.

CHANDNI Sudha is dead.

TOP RANI Oh. Are you sure?

CHANDNI She's not breathing.

TOP RANI My daughter is dead. May she be happy in the ever after. May she never open her legs again. *(pause)* Is that jeweller your customer?

CHANDNI Sudha is dead. Is that all you can…

TOP RANI Is the jeweller your customer or not?

CHANDNI Yes…

TOP RANI He's a very unhappy man.

CHANDNI About what? He goes mad every time I touch him. He brings me a gift every time he comes. Last time he got me a necklace the thickness of a dog leash. So there is no problem.

TOP RANI He's already paying you. Why the necklace?

CHANDNI Ask him.

TOP RANI Something tells me the answer is right here.

CHANDNI But he's very happy with me.

TOP RANI Then the problem lies in his happiness. What words of wisdom have you been whispering to him?

CHANDNI I don't have any wisdom to give.

TOP RANI goes to his wooden cupboard and removes a pack of cards. He walks back to CHANDNI.

TOP RANI Are you sure you did not disclose anything to the jeweller?

CHANDNI I'm sure.

TOP RANI *(chucking cards towards her)* I would like you to use the very subtle clues I am throwing your way. Are you sure there is nothing you have revealed?

> *CHANDNI tries to leave. TOP RANI throws her to the floor. He puts his foot on her chest.*

Think hard. I'm not afraid to lose one more daughter. *(pointing to the cage)* Replacements are not that hard to find.

CHANDNI I just told him... you do not pick cards... from the matka for the last bet of the year.

TOP RANI What makes you think that?

CHANDNI I made it up.

TOP RANI What else did you tell him?

CHANDNI Nothing.

> *He puts more pressure with his foot.*

TOP RANI What else did you tell him?

CHANDNI I told him that I knew how you called the closing number on that day.

TOP RANI Why in the name of prostitution did you say that?

CHANDNI He thought that I knew something and kept offering me the necklace if I gave him a tip. So I lied. I told him that this year you would decide the closing number based on which daughter earns the most money.

> *He lifts his foot off her.*

TOP RANI And that idiot believed you? The jeweller must have placed a huge bet with a bookie. Now he's calling me up to talk ill of the bookie because he doesn't want to pay up. If I intervene, then no money to pay. But his plan flopped double time. And you got a necklace on top of that. Go fetch it.

> *Exit CHANDNI.*

(to AARTI) Now, dear one. It's time we have a little talk. Do you know what we do here? This is a *kotha* where girls

rent their bodies to older men. Your own father tried to kill you. A speck of dust on his shirt sleeve that he flicked away straight into traffic. It's a small miracle that he died and you are alive, so take it that you're meant to be here. You start work tonight. It will distract you from your father's death. Chandni!

Enter CHANDNI with the chain.

I will keep the chain. As punishment, you will not step out of this brothel without my permission.

CHANDNI   I'm leaving for good.

> *TOP RANI digs his ear as if he did not hear correctly.*

I'm buying my freedom.

TOP RANI   My dear, even gold cannot take your place.

CHANDNI   You have Aarti now. She will grow into a beautiful woman.

TOP RANI   I will watch you die in this brothel, but you will never leave.

CHANDNI   What if you die first?

> *TOP RANI holds his heart. He staggers back and forth, slowly moving towards CHANDNI.*

TOP RANI   My own daughter... ooh it breaks my heart in two... no... three... no... twenty-three...

> *He suddenly grabs hold of CHANDNI's hair and pulls her to the floor. He pushes her face very close to the floor.*

What do you see down there?

CHANDNI   I... don't know...

TOP RANI   Look closely and you will see the roots of your prostitution. If you leave this brothel, you will die without roots. You cannot read, you cannot write. What will you do? Hah? Maybe you can get married. Indian men love virgins. You are my daughter. Now stay at home and act like one.

He lets her go. She stays on the ground. He pats her hair lovingly as he looks at AARTI.

(to AARTI) See? Our family is very close. I just can't let her go.

CHANDNI gets up. TOP RANI looks at AARTI.

Chandni. That foreign tourist who came last night. He's staying at Hotel Baaz, round the corner. Go tell him that I have an opportunity for him—a new girl, very young, needs breaking in. But if he mentions a word to anyone, tell him that even though he came from his country in a plane, he will go back in a box.

He violently kicks the cage bars.

Even smaller than this cage!

2.

Grant Road. December 31st. 8:00 p.m. GANTAAL is asleep. The white sheet covers him. The full moon shines on him. Enter SATTA. He is covered in blood. Shards of glass are stuck in his face.

SATTA I have a tip for you.

GANTAAL wakes up and looks at SATTA.

Are you listening? I have a tip.

GANTAAL You are dead.

SATTA That is why my tip is dead accurate.

GANTAAL What are you talking about?

SATTA I failed her, Gantaal. I failed my own child.

GANTAAL Why did you have to kill yourself?

SATTA It was either the car, or Khalil Bhai's knife. I wish Aarti were dead too. Why did she have to live?

GANTAAL It's too late now. Nothing can be done.

SATTA   They will turn my Aarti into a prostitute... my Aarti...
you must do something.

GANTAAL   This has nothing to do with me.

SATTA   Here is my tip. Do something. Otherwise you will have
to come home with me. *(pointing to the moon)* All bad people
stay there. You know that.

> *The moon moves towards SATTA. SATTA runs from it.*

It's coming for me. I have to go.

> *SATTA exits. A soft wind starts to blow and the
> white sheet flutters. The wind picks up momentum.
> GANTAAL gets up and the sheet slowly comes off
> him. It floats high in the air. He looks at the sheet and
> deliberates.*

GANTAAL   *(to Aroramanyu)* Aroramanyu, this is your wing.
Now take it to her and protect her from harm.

> *The wind rises to a crescendo and the sheet sails away
> across stage rising higher and higher.*

3.

> *The brothel. 8:00 p.m. A wind blows through the
> brothel. CHANDNI is at a clothesline. She is putting
> clothes into a dirty plastic bucket. There is a bedsheet on
> the line. It looks exactly like GANTAAL's sheet.*

CHANDNI   *(to AARTI)* Years ago, I was in that same cage. I was
just as stubborn as you are. Until Top Rani had a man sent
in.

> *The wind picks up momentum. The sheet rises high.
> AARTI watches it.*

But you are luckier than I was. I went to Hotel Baaz but the
foreign man has left.

> *The sheet floats high in the air. Enter TOP RANI. He
> watches as the sheet lands over the cage. AARTI pulls
> the sheet through the cage and covers herself.*

TOP RANI Don't get too used to covering yourself. If God had intended for us to wear clothes, we would be born with them. We only wear skin, little one. Do you understand? *(pause)* Chandni, explain the rules to her.

> *CHANDNI turns to leave.*

I want you to explain the rules to her.

CHANDNI You will be given two meals a day. You will never be allowed to leave this place for the rest of your life. This is your new home. Get used to it. If you cry, you will be beaten with a cricket bat. There will be no marks on your body. But your stomach will hurt. A constant thumping of the stomach will stop babies. We do not want babies.

> *CHANDNI is unable to go on. She exits.*

TOP RANI She left out the best part. Once in a while, you can listen to the radio. Did you understand everything that was just said?

> *She does not look his way. TOP RANI fetches the cricket bat and bangs it hard against the cage. AARTI sits up, petrified. Her hands shaking, she indicates that she would like to write something.*

What—you want to write?

> *She nods. He gets her a pencil and some scraps of paper. He gives it to her. She starts writing.*

I hope it's not a letter to your father. Postage will be expensive.

> *She hands him the paper. He reads from it.*

"My mother's sister will give money." I did not know this. Chandni is slacking in research. Where was this woman when I came to the hospital to take you? Hah? You were alone there. Your father was inside dying. No one will help you now. What does she do?

> *AARTI starts writing again. She gives him the paper. He reads.*

"Sweeper. Jeweller's shop. Grant Road."

(reading again) Jeweller's shop. At Grant Road.

> *TOP RANI smiles as though his mind has just solved an equation.*

(shouting) Chandni!

> *Enter CHANDNI.*

Ask her where her mother's sister works. Ask her. You will understand why.

CHANDNI Where does your mother's sister work?

TOP RANI In a jeweller's shop at Grant Road.

CHANDNI The same jeweller who...

TOP RANI Word of mouth is wonderful isn't it? I was wondering why that stupid father of hers was so sure that he would win. From prostitute to jeweller to sweeper to gambler. The Matka tip chain! And who pays in the end? A ten-year-old girl!

CHANDNI What have I done?

TOP RANI It is destiny. God willing, I will help her fulfill it tonight.

CHANDNI But the foreign man has left.

TOP RANI Are you sure?

CHANDNI He's gone.

> *He studies CHANDNI's face for a brief moment.*

TOP RANI *(to AARTI)* Sorry. No foreign university for you. But Indian education is also good. *(to CHANDNI)* Don't be upset. What you have done is most natural.

CHANDNI How?

TOP RANI One prostitute died. So you gave birth to another.

> *CHANDNI turns around to leave.*

Where are you going?

CHANDNI   To make preparations for Sudha's cremation.

TOP RANI   Be careful that *you* don't get burned.

> *She exits.*

(*to AARTI*) Chandni was my first prostitute. She was the same age as you when I had her broken in. God works in strange ways. He breaks you suddenly, when you least expect it. He takes every drop of life from you. Then one day you wake up stronger than before… like a tiger. No one can touch you then.

> *She gives him a piece of paper again.*

"Chance to win freedom." Freedom? No one is *free*. Look at me. I have money. I have long, strong muscles. But when I step into the street, even a stray dog gets more love than I do. No one is free.

> *She asks him to turn the paper around. He does. He reads.*

"Let us bet." This is turning into a very bad scene from a Hindi movie. But… if God wants you to be free, you will. Chandni!

> *CHANDNI enters with a sari in her hand. She stares at TOP RANI.*

CHANDNI   Take this.

> *She holds the sari out for TOP RANI.*

TOP RANI   What is it?

CHANDNI   It's what Sudha died in. Perhaps you'd like to wear it.

> *She thrusts the sari in his hands. TOP RANI caresses it.*

TOP RANI   I'll keep it. I'll save it for Aarti.

> *CHANDNI tries to take the sari back from him, but TOP RANI holds on.*

Do you remember yesterday's opening and closing numbers?

> *CHANDNI is still trying to tug the sari from his hands.*

CHANDNI Yes.

> *TOP RANI lets go. CHANDNI jerks back a little. He walks to the cupboard. He removes two blank cards from the cupboard, and a pencil. He hands the blank cards and pencil to CHANDNI but she does not take them.*

TOP RANI Now put that dead sari down and hold these cards. Write down the opening number on one card, and the closing number on the other.

> *She does.*

Now show me.

> *She shows the cards to TOP RANI.*

Now show her.

> *CHANDNI shows the cards to AARTI.*

Now show Him.

CHANDNI Who?

TOP RANI God. *(looking up)* Pay attention. A little girl is at stake.

> *He puts the cards in the matka.*

(to AARTI) The cards will decide your fate. If you pick the opening number, you will stay here and open your legs for the rest of your life. If you pick the closing number, your legs can remain closed. You will be free to go. Is it agreed?

> *She nods—yes.*

Then let us proceed. But I'm afraid I know how this is going to turn out.

> *He takes the matka to AARTI. AARTI closes her eyes. She collects her thoughts in her fist. She tries to throw them to the moon—to Aroramanyu. But TOP RANI prevents her from doing so.*

What are you doing? Just put your hand in and pull. Like Chandni.

> *AARTI puts one hand over her eyes and puts the other hand in the matka and removes a card. She looks at it in horror.*

What did you pull?

> *TOP RANI snatches the card from her hand.*

I knew it! These Hindi movies are misleading the public. They think someday they will be rescued.

> *He takes the card from her hand throws it back in the matka.*

Now for the victory dance!

> *TOP RANI claps his hands twice. A vulgar Hindi song comes on. It has a disco beat. TOP RANI does a eunuch dance that is also a parody of a Hindi movie dance number. The victory dance lasts for about a minute and a half. GANTAAL's voice can be heard from outside.*

GANTAAL Ten rupees only! Ten rupees only!

> *TOP RANI goes to the window.*

Show me your palm and you will come to no harm!

TOP RANI A fortune teller.

CHANDNI What an idiot. Coming to the red light district to tell people's fortunes.

TOP RANI He's looking here. This is a good sign. Today is a special day.

CHANDNI Why do you keep saying that?

TOP RANI You have a new sister. What could be more special?

GANTAAL Ten rupees only.

TOP RANI *(to CHANDNI)* You are also ten rupees only. Would you like to know your fortune?

> *CHANDNI shakes her head.*

(to AARTI) What about you?

> *AARTI does not respond. She just looks down at her feet. He claps his hands and calls GANTAAL up.*

Will the two of you stop behaving as if somebody just died?

> *Enter GANTAAL.*

GANTAAL Thank you for inviting me.

> *The moment AARTI hears GANTAAL's voice she looks up. He catches her eye for a second and then ignores her.*

TOP RANI This flower here is very interested in knowing her fortune.

GANTAAL Which flower?

TOP RANI This one. Here.

GANTAAL And what is the flower's name?

> *CHANDNI does not respond.*

TOP RANI Chandni.

> *TOP RANI goes to her and gently holds her by the hair.*

Chandni would like to ask you something.

CHANDNI What is the future like for me?

TOP RANI Wide open.

GANTAAL Show me your hand, Chandni. Don't be shy.

> *GANTAAL takes CHANDNI's hand. He smiles.*

You have a very long lifeline.

TOP RANI That is *exactly* what she wants to hear. "Hello, my name is Chandni. I am a prostitute of ninety years. Now you take off your pants while I take out my teeth."

GANTAAL You see this lump here? That is your good deed pocket. The mound is very high. It means you are a good person.

> *TOP RANI slaps CHANDNI's hand out of the way.*

TOP RANI My turn.

GANTAAL Money first.

> *TOP RANI gives GANTAAL the money. Then he extends his hand. GANTAAL takes it.*

Your good deed pocket is empty. But there is something else. Oh, this is strange, very strange.

TOP RANI What.

GANTAAL Your lifeline. It stops.

TOP RANI Everyone's lifeline stops.

GANTAAL But there is a reversal in yours.

TOP RANI What did you say?

GANTAAL Your lifeline suddenly changes direction. It moves in reverse.

TOP RANI What does that mean?

GANTAAL It means that you will soon start a new life. Very different from the one you are leading. Perhaps a reversal of fortunes. Or a change of heart.

TOP RANI How do you know this?

GANTAAL Your hand speaks to me.

TOP RANI Then ask my hand this: Will my cock grow back?

> *GANTAAL looks at TOP RANI in surprise.*

I'm serious.

GANTAAL Why would it?

TOP RANI The Myth of Merit. It is a time-honoured custom.

GANTAAL We have many stupid customs.

TOP RANI I know. A eunuch is one of them.

> *GANTAAL nods towards the cage.*

GANTAAL What about her? She is extremely custom-made.

TOP RANI Are you here to tell my fortune or to get lucky?

GANTAAL I wish to buy her from you.

TOP RANI What makes you think she is for sale?

GANTAAL If she is in a cage, it means she has not been tamed. Has she?

TOP RANI What are you willing to pay?

GANTAAL Nothing.

TOP RANI Good answer. Good answer. But what does it mean?

GANTAAL If I help you become a man again, you help me become a man again.

TOP RANI I don't need your help.

GANTAAL Then why are you still in a sari?

> *TOP RANI goes towards him in a threatening manner.*

I mean the Myth of Merit.

TOP RANI What about it?

GANTAAL It is not a myth.

> *He exits. AARTI lifts her head from the sheet and watches him leave.*

TOP RANI Today is a special day indeed.

CHANDNI What do you mean?

TOP RANI The Myth of Merit.

CHANDNI Surely you don't believe in that rubbish. They are called myths because they're not true.

TOP RANI A myth is a forgotten truth. In my village there lived a girl just like Aarti—no voice, no parents, nothing. All day she would sit in a little clearing just outside the forest with her head in her knees. One day a tiger came into the clearing. Everyone ran. Except the little girl. She held up her hand and said something to the tiger—no words, but she said something. The great beast roared and roared, but it never touched her. It walked back into the forest.

CHANDNI   What does that have to do with Aarti?

TOP RANI   Has anyone touched her so far?

CHANDNI   No.

TOP RANI   Then she has proved that myths *can* be true. The myth goes that children who have no voice… have God speaking for them.

CHANDNI   But you are a eunuch. That will never change.

TOP RANI   Don't be so sure.

> *He walks to the cupboard. From a secret compartment he takes out a glass jar covered with a black cloth.*

CHANDNI   What's that?

TOP RANI   My graduation present.

> *CHANDNI puts her hand out to see what lies beneath the black cloth. TOP RANI grabs her hand.*

When I was ten years old, my father sent me to the city to work as a servant boy. My master sold this little servant boy to a band of eunuchs even though I was not *his* to sell. The coward had gambling debts to pay. One night, they castrated me in my master's kitchen. From then on, I dressed like hijras do and learnt their ways. I made money for them by begging at traffic lights, singing at weddings, and by being a prostitute myself. At age twenty, I had completed all the requirements and training of being a eunuch. I was allowed to branch out on my own. In this glass jar, they kept what they had cut off.

> *CHANDNI looks down at her feet.*

Go ahead. Take a look. I'm proud of it. It's my letter of recommendation. It is also why I believe I can still become whole.

4.

Grant Road. 8:45 p.m. GANTAAL is sleeping. SATTA
enters. He is trapped inside the moon. He wakes
GANTAAL up.

SATTA You must be a good father to her. There are certain
things she likes. When her hair is wet, you must comb it back
immediately. The knots are hard to remove once her hair
dries. At night, she sometimes cries in her sleep. She dreams
about her mother. Don't wake her up. One night I swear I
heard her speak in her sleep. She actually spoke. She loves to
watch movies, Gantaal. Take her to the movies. And let her
know that I love her. Tell her how sorry I am. Tell her that
her mother and I are together again. It may not be true, but it
will make her happy.

GANTAAL Where will I keep her? The streets are no place for a
child. I cannot be responsible for her.

SATTA You have no choice. She likes you too much. She will
be a good daughter to you. She will look after you when you
are old.

GANTAAL I am already old.

SATTA As long as there is breath in you, you are young.
Remember that.

GANTAAL How the hell do I save her?

SATTA I have to go now. I place Aarti in your hands. Goodbye,
my friend.

GANTAAL Wait!

SATTA and the moon disappear. Everything is quiet.

How the hell do I save her?

He opens the trunk.

Maybe I should ask Polly. Hah? Why don't you speak? Say
something. What can a poor fortune teller do? All my life I
have tricked people. What trick can I pull this time? Maybe

I am asking the wrong person. But who to ask then? Who to ask?

Enter CHANDNI. GANTAAL stands up. They face each other.

5.

The brothel. Close to midnight.

TOP RANI After they cut me, the pain took me in and out of this world. The mud was washed away, and replaced by oil to clean the wound. They made me go without food or water for three days so I would not urinate. On the fourth day, they fed me milk, and it left my body through a thin tube that was placed in a hole. That was all they left me: A hole. I used to wake up in the middle of the night groping. I'd feel my groin again and again in the hope that I might find something. In the bazaar, when no one was looking, I'd feel. In the kitchen when no one was cooking, I'd feel. I'd feel *nothing*. But then I realized that suffering can be a beautiful thing. If I welcomed it, it would make me worthy of being whole.

He holds his crotch.

For true works of art are born only from great suffering.

He lights a match.

Fire. When we are cremated, fire is what takes us from this world to the next. It is New Year's Eve. Each year, at this time I light a match. As I watch the flame burn, I can hear Surya scream.

He listens.

Can you hear anything?

Silence.

Surya has *never* been silent. It means his passage to the spirit world is complete. And I will pull a king.

GANTAAL enters. TOP RANI blows out the match.

Who let you in?

GANTAAL You did.

TOP RANI I'm in no mood for deeper meanings.

GANTAAL I'm talking about the Myth of Merit. *(pause)* What is the purpose of being a man? Of enabling a woman to have a child. So the cycle of birth can continue. If you do not have a cock, is it possible to have a child?

TOP RANI No.

GANTAAL Now what if you had a child?

TOP RANI So what if I had one?

GANTAAL It would mean you have a cock.

TOP RANI Yes.

GANTAAL But you *do* have a child.

TOP RANI I do?

> *GANTAAL looks towards the cage.*

Yes, she is my daughter. Even Chandni is my daughter. I have many daughters. I should have many cocks. What are you getting at?

GANTAAL The Myth of Merit works *backwards*. If you have a daughter, it means you are *already* worthy.

TOP RANI So if I am already worthy, I should be whole. Do I wait for my cock to grow back?

GANTAAL Nothing will *grow*. Your part can only be re-attached. But it would be cruel of me to even hope that you still have your part.

> *TOP RANI walks to the cupboard and takes out the glass jar. He holds it like a prize.*

What is that?

TOP RANI Top Rani. Part Two.

> *GANTAAL lifts the cloth and takes a look.*

GANTAAL Oh my God…

TOP RANI Horrible, no?

GANTAAL No…

TOP RANI Horrible…

GANTAAL There is a chance then. A very *small* chance.

TOP RANI I will take it.

GANTAAL Then fulfill this condition: the little girl must truly accept you as her father. If she does not accept you, nothing can be done.

TOP RANI Why?

GANTAAL The bond must be real. She must be attached to you.

TOP RANI So *this* can be attached to me?

> *GANTAAL nods.*

If we were in any other country, I would laugh in your face. But here, with a thousand gods, at least one will be in charge of cocks.

GANTAAL Be good to the girl and she will accept you.

> *CHANDNI enters.*

TOP RANI *(to CHANDNI)* I told you not to leave this brothel without my permission.

CHANDNI I was at the cremation site. It will be a few hours before we can begin.

TOP RANI I shall attend. I will need a white pant and shirt.

CHANDNI Men's clothing?

TOP RANI I told you today is special. Let Aarti out.

> *He gives her the key to the cage, which is around his neck.*

CHANDNI What?

TOP RANI I said let her out. She will eat with me.

> *CHANDNI opens the cage door. But AARTI does not come out.*

CHANDNI   She's not coming out.

TOP RANI   Aarti, come out. I will not hurt you. I promise.

> *He walks over to the cage.*

Aarti, your father is here. Don't you want to see your own father?

CHANDNI   What are you doing?

> *TOP RANI raises his hand to silence her. He takes the key back from CHANDNI. He bends down to talk to AARTI. AARTI leans forward eager to see her father.*

TOP RANI   I am your father.

> *In anger, AARTI hits TOP RANI's hand. The glass jar is in the same hand. The jar falls to the floor. There is a resounding smash as the jar breaks.*

No!

> *TOP RANI scrambles to retrieve the remains on the floor. CHANDNI quickly shuts the cage door fearing that TOP RANI will harm AARTI.*

It is destiny! You are meant to be a prostitute!

CHANDNI   It was an accident.

TOP RANI   She destroyed it! Now I will destroy her!

GANTAAL   But there are other ways.

TOP RANI   You're only interested in the girl!

GANTAAL   True.

TOP RANI   Then break her in right now. I don't want money. I want her to suffer.

GANTAAL   I...

TOP RANI   Either you agree or I will give her to any one of the taxi drivers downstairs.

GANTAAL I will do it. But you must leave this place for half an hour.

TOP RANI What for?

GANTAAL I want to be alone with the girl.

TOP RANI I will grant you the request. If I stay on, I will kill the girl. You have ten minutes. It will be midnight soon. *(to CHANDNI)* She's quite young, isn't she?

CHANDNI I'm so glad you can count.

TOP RANI You're not saying much. A little girl will be raped and you're not taking it to heart?

CHANDNI It was done to me as well. Let's go.

TOP RANI You're not going to stop me?

CHANDNI Are you testing me?

TOP RANI Should I be testing you?

CHANDNI No.

> *He takes a hard look at CHANDNI to see if she is up to anything. He throws some money into the cage.*

TOP RANI Never work for free.

> *They exit. TOP RANI remains in the shadows. GANTAAL rushes to the cage. AARTI reaches for GANTAAL through the cage bars.*

GANTAAL Don't be afraid, my angel.

> *He tries to open the cage.*

It's locked!

> *TOP RANI steps forward holding the key.*

TOP RANI She's a burning flower, isn't she?

GANTAAL Yes, I cannot wait.

> *TOP RANI gives GANTAAL the key. GANTAAL turns to unlock the cage. TOP RANI picks up the stone*

*phallus and strikes GANTAAL on the back of the head.
GANTAAL falls to the floor. TOP RANI ties him to the
cage with rope.*

TOP RANI From the beginning, it's all about betting. From the
time of birth. Will it be a boy or will it be a girl? If you start
betting with the unborn, then naturally the rest of your life
will also be a gamble. But every once in a while God throws
us a googly: a eunuch is born. And God, the greatest bookie
of them all, looks down and laughs: "It's a sin to gamble," he
says. But it's not a sin to take that which is rightfully mine.
At midnight when I put my hand in the matka, I am *meant*
to pull a king. For I was not born a eunuch. I must honour
God's wishes and live in the form he chose for me.

He holds the matka in his hands.

Ten minutes to "Pull the King."

He caresses the matka. He sees that it is dirty.

Why has it not been washed? Chandni!

*He goes to the inside of the brothel with the matka.
GANTAAL slowly regains consciousness. TOP RANI
comes back without the matka.*

(to AARTI) You've already seen one father die. How do you
wish to see this one go?

AARTI stares at him.

How do you wish to see this one go?

GANTAAL Same way the first one did.

TOP RANI Should I throw you in traffic?

GANTAAL Matka. Let us make a bet. If I guess the closing
number, she goes free.

TOP RANI We are betting on how you die. Plus, tonight no
closing number. We play "Pull the King."

GANTAAL That is a stupid game.

TOP RANI What did you say?

GANTAAL "Pull the King" is a stupid game. No one ever wins because you are cheating.

TOP RANI I am *not* cheating! I *want* to pull a king!

> *TOP RANI regrets uttering these words. GANTAAL notices.*

GANTAAL I believe you. I know that you are not cheating.

TOP RANI And who told you that?

GANTAAL Polly the Punter.

TOP RANI Polly the Punter?

GANTAAL He is capable of guessing the opening and closing numbers of Matka.

TOP RANI If that were the case, why are you so poor? You should have been rich knowing the Matka numbers in advance.

GANTAAL Polly only helps those in *real* need. If he predicts the numbers for financial gain, he will lose his powers.

TOP RANI *(dismissing him)* Cha!

GANTAAL Polly the Punter said that you will *never* pull a king.

TOP RANI You're lying.

GANTAAL Bring him to me and I shall prove to you that I am not.

TOP RANI Where does this Polly the Punter live?

GANTAAL In my trunk.

TOP RANI In your trunk?

GANTAAL Polly is my parrot.

TOP RANI A parrot? Why would I listen to a worthless parrot?

GANTAAL Because the two of you have something in common.

TOP RANI And what would that be?

GANTAAL Your name. Because of his gift, Polly the Punter is also known as "The Matka King."

TOP RANI What?

GANTAAL That's what the gamblers of this city call him.

TOP RANI And he said I will *never* pull a king?

GANTAAL Correct.

TOP RANI Why?

GANTAAL Ask him yourself.

TOP RANI Where is your trunk?

GANTAAL Just outside.

TOP RANI Chandni!

> *She enters.*

You must get Polly.

CHANDNI Polly?

TOP RANI His parrot.

GANTAAL It's in my trunk, just outside. When you get there, keep the trunk open, just a little, for a minute, and let the smell of the city seep in. Only then will my parrot sleep. Otherwise it will escape.

> *CHANDNI exits.*

TOP RANI Hurry up! It's almost midnight! *(to himself)* If he is a king I must listen. Polly will tell me what I am doing wrong. I cannot wait another year.

> *Enter CHANDNI with a small bag slung around her shoulder.*

Where is my king? Let me see him.

> *She takes Polly out from the bag.*

No... he's not even a real parrot...

He grabs Polly and flings him against the cage bars. He moves towards the cage. CHANDNI steps in his way.

CHANDNI It's midnight.

He stops. He looks for the matka.

TOP RANI Where is the matka? Get it right now.

CHANDNI exits. TOP RANI goes to the cupboard to get the pack of cards. He opens a new pack of cards and takes out his customary blindfold as well. He blindfolds himself and kneels on the floor.

I shall no longer be called Top Rani. I shall go by the name my father gave me. Vijay. Victory.

CHANDNI enters and puts the matka in front of him. TOP RANI throws the cards into the matka. As he does so, we hear the hiss of a cobra. TOP RANI freezes. He takes his blindfold off and looks into the matka. He cannot take his eyes off the matka. Eyes still on the matka, he hands the cage key to CHANDNI.

Free them.

CHANDNI What?

TOP RANI If you ever set foot in this brothel again, I'll kill you.

CHANDNI You're just letting us go?

TOP RANI Trees, fire, mud, and *betrayal*. Now get out.

CHANDNI goes to the cage to free GANTAAL and AARTI. They exit.

Surya was right. What is a cobra if not a king?

He lets his long hair loose. He takes his bangles off. He rubs off his make-up. He slowly puts his hand into the matka. The cobra strikes. But he still keeps his hand in. The cobra strikes again. He slowly falls to the floor.

When you die… everybody is the same… neither man nor woman… neither woman nor man…

He waits for death to come. There is the sound of fire.
The dark shadow of Surya looms behind him. Surya has
come to take TOP RANI to the spirit world.

EPILOGUE

The sound of people speaking in different Indian
languages—bits of Hindi, Marathi, Gujarati and so on.
The tone is forceful and congested, as if a heated debate
is taking place. SATTA stands alone on stage.

SATTA The moment I came to the spirit world, I looked for
my wife everywhere. I called her name a thousand times—
Shanti, Shanti… but there was no response. I understand
why. She's in a different place. When you die, your own
conscience takes you to the place you deserve to go to. A
man who gambles his own daughter away isn't a man.
He's a eunuch. Testicles notwithstanding. If you gave such
a person a moral compass, it would point straight to his
heart and his heart would tell him what a coward he's been.
(pause) Right now, I'm part of a reception committee. Half of
Bombay is here—gamblers, bookies, prostitutes. Even Sudha.
There are scores to settle, questions to ask. So you'll have
to excuse us. We're awaiting the arrival of a very important
guest. We have lots to talk about.

The voices rise again to a frenzied crescendo.

END OF PLAY

BOMBAY BLACK

Anita Majumdar as Apsara
photo by John Lauener

Bombay Black premiered in January 2006 at the Theatre Centre, Toronto, with the following company:

Deena Aziz	Padma
Anita Majumdar	Apsara
Sanjay Talwar	Kamal
Brian Quirt	Director
Andrea Romaldi	Assistant Director
Camellia Koo	Set Designer
Rebecca Picherack	Lighting Designer
Suba Sankaran	Composer/Sound Designer
Nova Bhattacharya	Choreographer
Stephen Lalande	Production Manager
Greg Poulin	Technical Director (Theatre Centre)
Jung Hye Kim	Design Assistant
Camellia Koo &	
Jung Hye Kim	Scenic Artists
Isaac Thomas	Stage Manager

Bombay Black was commissioned and developed by Nightswimming Theatre and produced by Cahoots Theatre Projects. It was workshopped and given a public reading at On the Verge, 2005 at the National Arts Centre, Ottawa.

The playwright is extremely grateful to the Canada Council for the Arts for its generous support.

ACT ONE

1.

Evening. The stage is dark. The sound of a woman's anklets beating against the floor in the darkness. This is APSARA. Only she can be seen. She performs the Dance of Empowerment. The music and the dance should have a modern sensibility. The dance APSARA performs borrows from the courtesans of Ancient India as well as present day Bombay bar girls. The idea is that she is sucking the energy of the man she is performing for, all the while pretending that she is serving him. The dance progressively becomes more and more seductive. After a minute of dance, a voice:

PADMA Make eye contact with the man. Then lower your eyes from time to time as though you cannot bear the strength of his gaze. This will make him feel powerful. Go slower when you reveal your thighs. Make the man wait. Punish him. That's the true purpose of dance, my dear—to turn men into vegetables.

> *APSARA stops dancing. Lights. PADMA is revealed.*

What's wrong? Why did you stop? I thought you liked vegetables. *(pause)* I've been meaning to ask you: isn't it time you learned some new moves? It's quite charming, your little dance, but…. I need you to swivel your hips more. Dance more like a *tart* and less like an *artist*. Yes, that's it. Be more tartish. Are you listening?

APSARA To every word. Your gloom is so reassuring.

PADMA And make sure you oil your hair every night. It needs more shine.

APSARA It's too much work.

PADMA Being a tart is hard work. Requires dedication and commitment. That's the problem with you young people. You don't take anything seriously. Now get some rest. You have an appointment at nine.

APSARA Who is it tonight?

PADMA A new client.

APSARA From where?

PADMA He's from the suburbs—Malad or Mulund, one of those—I can't remember. Anyway, I spoke to him over the phone. He has no reference so I'm charging him three thousand rupees—not bad for an hour of dance, hah? Now. Let's go for a walk.

APSARA No.

PADMA Fifteen minutes. That's all. The sun's about to set. Whenever I watch the sun go down, I always ask myself, "What if the sun doesn't show up tomorrow?" Such a massive universe, one wrong turn and the sun is lost. That's why I always thank the sun each day. To make it feel appreciated.

APSARA You need to make some friends, mother.

PADMA I have friends. The butcher's my friend. What's his name...

APSARA The butcher cannot be counted as a friend.

PADMA But I bought a knife from him. What's his name... Hanif Bhai, that's it. We had a friendly exchange once. "What nice meat you have," I said, and he replied, "It's all in the knife, Madam. The way you cut meat is important." I have friends.

APSARA You can't go for a walk with the butcher.

PADMA That's why I'm asking you to go with me.

APSARA I don't want to.

PADMA Fine. Then I won't go either. There will be no one to thank the sun. If the sun doesn't rise tomorrow, it will be your fault. The whole world will be plunged into darkness because you are a selfish little bitch. (pause) Is it such a task for you to spend time with your dying mother?

APSARA I wasn't aware you were dying.

PADMA I might, I might. Anything can happen. Heart attacks come when you least expect them. They are like surprise tests. You'll be having a normal day, you know, frying fish or boiling eggs or oiling your hair when suddenly your heart will skip a beat. Then you'll think you've imagined it, but just to make sure you will concentrate, and that concentration will make you nervous, and out of nervousness your heart will skip again, and then you will tell yourself, "Oh God, it's happening, I'm getting a massive heart attack." Then just to torture you, nothing will happen for at least ten minutes, and then you'll relax again, and *that's* when the pain shoots through you like a local train, and you know you have only a few seconds left on earth, and you thank your stars you've been good to the sun because God will send you straight to hell and you'll need the sun to light the way.

APSARA You're a beacon of hope today, mother.

PADMA Yes, my dear, I know. By the way, I had a new costume made for you. It reveals your stomach more. Every man that comes in here wants to lick your stomach and thighs. So we must open the door a little more. Not a lot, just a little.

APSARA How thoughtful of you.

PADMA More meat, more heat. *(pause)* Apsara, what's the matter with you today? You're not your usual, unintelligent self. You look like you're actually contemplating something. Even during the dance, you were distracted.

APSARA It's nothing.

PADMA Tell me. You know how soothing I can be.

APSARA It's just that I can smell country liquor. You know, the kind father used to drink. I smell country liquor made out of orange peels and leather. It's been years since I've got that smell.

PADMA It's probably the sea. It's called the Arabian Sea because it smells like a camel.

APSARA It's not the sea. My father smells nothing like the sea. You know that. It's that thick, heavy smell…

PADMA First of all, your father's probably dead. No one in the village knows where he is and it's been years since anyone's seen him. But if he's alive, we're in a city of eighteen million people. He'll never find us.

APSARA What if he does?

PADMA I won't let him near you. I promise. *(pause)* Now let's go—the sun is waiting.

2.

Night. PADMA is preparing the apartment for the customer's arrival. She fluffs the cushions on the swing, dims the lights to set a mood. There is a knock on the door. PADMA opens the door. It is KAMAL. He is unseen.

KAMAL Is this apartment 4-A? Ocean Heights?

PADMA Yes.

KAMAL I spoke to you over the phone.

PADMA You're late.

KAMAL I'm sorry. It's just that…

PADMA Why are you panting? We're only on the fourth floor.

KAMAL Yes, but there's no lift… and the stairs are very steep.

PADMA Come in.

KAMAL walks in. His manner of walking suggests that he is blind.

Are you blind?

KAMAL Yes.

There is a long silence.

I apologize.

PADMA Would you like me to help you?

KAMAL Yes, please.

He offers her his hand. But she does not take it.

PADMA Keep walking straight for four feet. Then turn left about one foot. There's a swing. Sit on it.

He finds the swing.

Don't you people normally use a cane?

He sits.

KAMAL I lost my cane. The footpath is dug up just outside your building. I think I might have tripped over some wires.

PADMA Yes, yes. Telephone wires. Those phone company dogs are always digging. So many cross connections because of that. The other day I was on the line with a client and this little girl enters the conversation—she was trying to call her mathematics teacher. So I said to her, "Listen, little one, there's no use studying. Only your *body* will be of use." She started yelling for her mother. I quickly put the phone down. Some children are just not ready for the truth. Anyway—you were saying?

KAMAL Er… nothing. I wasn't saying anything.

PADMA You lost your cane.

KAMAL Yes. I lost my cane because I tripped over telephone wires. That's why I'm late.

PADMA Did you fall?

KAMAL No.

PADMA Were you robbed?

KAMAL I'm fine.

PADMA Good. Then I'll take the money first.

He reaches into his pocket and hands her a wad of money.

KAMAL No need to count. Fresh from the bank.

PADMA Lovely. Before we begin, let me explain the rules to you.

KAMAL You make it sound like a jail.

PADMA Apsara must be safe.

KAMAL Apsara. Beautiful name.

PADMA Bombay's Celestial Nymph.

KAMAL That's not what her name means.

PADMA I *know* what her name means.

KAMAL Apsara. Water that moves. A literal translation.

PADMA As I said, you need to know the rules. First and foremost: This is not a brothel.

KAMAL I'm aware of that.

PADMA That's what they all say. So allow me to get it through your thick skull. In a way it's good that you are blind. You people are acute listeners. This is *not* a brothel. There will be no touching. At all. She will not touch you. You will not touch her. Is that clear?

KAMAL No problem.

PADMA If at any point you do touch her, your hands will be broken with an iron rod. There are one-way mirrors. So I can see you, but you can't see me. A concept you're more than familiar with.

KAMAL Understood.

PADMA Any questions?

KAMAL No.

PADMA I have one.

KAMAL Go ahead.

PADMA What pleasure does a blind man get from dance?

KAMAL None whatsoever.

PADMA Then why do this?

KAMAL Tax write-off.

PADMA You look suspicious. Do you work for the police?

KAMAL No, Madam.

PADMA If you do, you're wasting your time. The ACP is our client. He loves Apsara.

KAMAL The Assistant Commissioner of Police is your client?

PADMA He loves to watch her dance. He requests the same bloody song each time he comes. He's an odd fellow. Doesn't smoke, doesn't drink… sips orange juice as Apsara dances. But he's a kind man. He said if I'm ever in any trouble, I should call him. So whatever department you're from, you're wasting your time.

KAMAL I work for no one.

PADMA What do you do for a living?

KAMAL I sell books.

PADMA You sell books. And you can afford to pay three thousand rupees.

KAMAL I sell *lots* of books.

PADMA I'll have to check you.

KAMAL What for?

PADMA I don't know. A knife, maybe. Stand up.

He does. She frisks him.

No I.D.? Where's your wallet?

KAMAL I don't carry one.

PADMA What's your name?

KAMAL I don't pay three thousand rupees to reveal my name.

PADMA So you're married.

KAMAL For many years.

PADMA   Don't worry. We don't blackmail. Our reputation is very good.

KAMAL   That's why I'm here.

PADMA   Now I did not mention this over the phone, but we offer cocaine as well. We charge extra for that.

KAMAL   No thank you.

PADMA   I can assure you the quality is perfect. Movie stars come here especially for that.

> *KAMAL shakes his head.*

Perhaps something low grade then—to match your personality? May I suggest some Bombay Black?

KAMAL   Bombay Black. What's that?

PADMA   A local drug made from hashish and shoe polish.

KAMAL   Sounds delicious. But no.

PADMA   One last question then. Are you vegetarian or non-vegetarian?

KAMAL   What difference?

PADMA   If you want to eat. Maybe your wife's a bad cook.

KAMAL   I'm vegetarian.

PADMA   A blind vegetarian. You poor man.

> *She walks away.*

KAMAL   Madam.

PADMA   Yes?

KAMAL   Put the lights off. I want complete darkness.

PADMA   What for?

KAMAL   When I meet a woman for the first time, I want her to see me the same way I see her.

> *PADMA puts the lights off and exits. APSARA enters. We hear her anklets in the dark. KAMAL stands in the*

centre of the room. He walks towards the door in the darkness. We hear the door open and close. APSARA puts the lights on. KAMAL is gone.

3.

APSARA is seated on the swing. PADMA opens the door to the room very slowly. She is surprised to find that APSARA is alone.

PADMA   Is he in the bathroom?

APSARA   No.

PADMA   Where is he then?

APSARA   I have no idea.

PADMA   What happened?

APSARA   Nothing happened. He just left. He walked out the moment I entered the room.

PADMA   You did not dance for him?

APSARA   I entered. The lights were off. Then I heard him walk towards the door. By the time I put the lights on, he had gone.

PADMA   That's strange. Perhaps you made him sad.

APSARA   How?

PADMA   You have that gift. Maybe his wife was a dancer, and she died in a car accident while he was driving—that explains his loss of sight—and he feels guilty, tremendously guilty, but at the same time he wants to be with her again, and since he's blind all he needs to do is be in the presence of a dancer, and the rest is in his mind—you become someone else, his wife, a lady named Sharmila or Shabana or something.

APSARA   That's quite a story.

PADMA When your own story is a piece of shit, you tell someone else's.

APSARA Why not re-dream your own story instead?

PADMA How futile that would be. Like an artist trying to paint the same picture twice.

APSARA In any case, I hope that's not the blind man's story.

PADMA Don't feel sorry for him.

APSARA He's the first blind person I've met.

PADMA He's not a person. He's a man. At the end of the day, he's a man. His blindness does not make him compassionate. Or valiant. Or worthy of love.

> *APSARA gets up.*

Where are you going?

APSARA To my room. Your optimism is infectious.

> *PADMA's cell phone rings. It is tucked in the folds of her sari. She picks up. She listens.*

PADMA Yes… okay then… nine tomorrow. *(to APSARA)* It's the blind vegetarian. He wants to see you again.

APSARA What for? Is he just going to throw away his money again?

PADMA Oh don't be so harsh on yourself. He's not *throwing* it away. You provide a valuable service, my dear. All these men who come here have wives who are ugly old bags, who, if they tried to dance, would have the effect of an enema. So hold your head up. Be proud. You are of *some* worth. Not a lot. Just a little.

4.

> *Morning. APSARA is asleep on the ground. The sun shines on APSARA's face. There is the crackling sound of a fire. The chanting of prayers. APSARA is extremely*

uneasy. PADMA enters carrying a shopping bag. She wakes her daughter up.

PADMA   Apsara... Apsara...

> *APSARA sits up. She is disoriented.*

Did you spend the whole night on the floor? I've told you not to sleep on the floor. You'll catch a cold.

APSARA   I had that dream again. I'm walking round a fire, there's smoke in my eyes, and I'm crying.

PADMA   Stop having that dream. Dream about something positive. Your father is walking down an empty road. Suddenly a car races towards him. Its brakes have failed. There is the look of terror on your father's face. But he manages to step out of harm's way in the nick of time. He looks skywards and thanks God for saving him. *(pause)* Then a truck appears out of nowhere and flattens the bastard. That's the kind of dream that is soothing.

APSARA   This time my dream was different. I was crying out to you. That's never happened before.

PADMA   I'm going to the market. Do you want anything?

APSARA   Why was I crying out to you?

PADMA   Apsara, please. I've just had my tea. Don't ask me morose questions just after my morning tea. It's about the only time I can barely manage to stay neutral. Now make yourself some breakfast. Don't starve while I'm gone.

> *She exits. A few seconds later, there is a knock on the door. APSARA opens the door.*

You?

> *It is KAMAL.*

KAMAL   May I come in?

APSARA   What are you doing here?

KAMAL   It's nine o'clock. I had called last night and fixed an appointment at nine.

APSARA That's nine at night.

KAMAL Morning and night look the same through my eyes.

APSARA I can't dance for you in the morning.

KAMAL I don't want you to dance.

　　　　He starts walking towards the swing.

　　(imitating PADMA) "Keep walking straight for four feet. Then turn left about one foot. There's a swing. Sit on it." Your mother is absolutely charming.

APSARA You can't just come in like that.

　　　　He sits on the swing.

KAMAL I haven't eaten a thing all night.

APSARA I'm sorry, but you'll have to leave.

KAMAL Are you going to deny a blind man food? *(pause)* I spent the night outside your house.

APSARA What for?

KAMAL Not right outside your door. I wouldn't do that. I slept by the sea wall. I live in the suburbs and I had to be here first thing in the morning. It's wonderful to wake up by the sea, especially here. The voices of beggars, stray dogs, pigeons, some roadside radio playing old Hindi songs.

APSARA If you spent the night outside, where did you call from last night? It would be hard for you to find a public telephone around here.

KAMAL Oh, I called from your neighbour's apartment. I told your neighbours that my car had broken down and I needed to call my mechanic. I dialed your number and said, "Hello, it's the blind man. I'd like to make an appointment at nine." Then after your mother hung up I said, "Can you please ask someone to pick me up outside Ocean Heights? The engine has stalled. Again."

APSARA The blind don't drive, you know.

KAMAL Your neighbours didn't seem to mind. They're a nice old couple.

APSARA We don't speak to them much.

KAMAL That's what the old woman said: "Unfriendly lot. God knows what business those people are in. Whole night strange men come to their house." Then the old man added, "I once saw the Assistant Commissioner of Police." They're a nice old couple. He even put on the radio for me until my mechanic came and picked me up.

APSARA What mechanic? There was no mechanic.

KAMAL That's what I thought. We were listening to the radio when the old man suddenly put the radio off. "Your mechanic's here," he said. I almost blurted out that there was no mechanic, but he went on: "I heard the car horn. My hearing's very sharp." So I had to leave.

APSARA Look—what do you want?

KAMAL Eggs would be nice.

APSARA A cup of tea. My mother just made some. That's all you get. Then you'll have to come back tonight.

KAMAL Five spoons of sugar, please.

APSARA Five? You want diabetes?

KAMAL Oh God, no. Diabetes leads to blindness.

APSARA I'll get your tea.

She exits. He talks to her loudly.

KAMAL I love this area, you know. Apollo Bunder, isn't it? Wonder where the name is from. Anyway, like I said, I just love it here. I was talking to this little beggar last night by the sea wall. Her name was Mangal. I always thought it was a man's name. Anyway, I asked her to describe the area for me, you know, since I can't see. She said, "I can see boats on the water, there are little boats and big boats but just now since it is night they are all silent, and I can see a lighthouse and the light is on otherwise the boats will bang, and I can

see men selling boiled eggs and bananas, and I am getting
hungry, so that will be five rupees." Can you imagine? So I
said, "No money, sorry. I spent it all on this dancer in that
building opposite whose horrible mother charges three
thousand rupees!" So she said, "Three thousand rupees for
dance? Are you mad?" *(pause)* I must be, no?

> *She returns with a cup of tea. She hands him the cup.*
> *He drinks.*

It's luke-warm. Chai should be hot. But it'll do. I really did
spend the night outside. I even got a massage in the night.

APSARA   You shouldn't have done that.

KAMAL   Why not? My body was aching. The massage was
superb. And cheap. So why not?

APSARA   Because sometimes massages are given by lepers.

KAMAL   What?

APSARA   And you are blind…

KAMAL   Lepers?

APSARA   The stumps of their hands work those pressure points
quite well, don't they?

KAMAL   Are you serious?

APSARA   Now quietly sip your tea.

KAMAL   I have something important to tell you. But I wanted to
wait until your mother was out of the house.

APSARA   What is it?

KAMAL   I will reveal something to you that will change your
life. But first we must get to know each other.

> *He drinks his tea.*

APSARA   Why would I agree?

KAMAL   Because you love me.

APSARA   Really.

KAMAL You're worried about my health. I like that in a woman. You put less than five spoons of sugar in my tea. Good for you.

APSARA Look, we can continue this tonight.

KAMAL Then I must get going. Your neighbour's house. To thank him for his generosity last night.

> *He gets up.*

Don't tell your mother I came here.

APSARA Why not?

KAMAL I don't trust her.

APSARA And why is that?

KAMAL Because in all these years, she hasn't told you a thing about me.

> *KAMAL exits. APSARA watches him closely as he leaves.*

5.

> *PADMA has just returned from the market.*

PADMA It looks like you haven't moved at all since I left. Did you eat anything?

APSARA No. What did you bring from the market?

PADMA Cauliflower, cabbage, lettuce. And some fresh meat for the eagles.

APSARA You have to stop feeding the eagles. Every time our building council has a meeting, they complain about you tossing chunks of meat out of the window.

PADMA I don't *toss* chunks of meat out of the window. That's uncivilized. I wait for the eagles to collect them from my hand. Now that's a good breed of bird. The general of all birds. They see red and they swoop. *(pause)* Whose cup of tea is that?

APSARA   Mine.

PADMA   In all these years, you haven't touched a drop of tea.

APSARA   You drive me to drink, mother.

PADMA   Don't be smart, Apsara. Someone was here.

APSARA   The blind man.

PADMA   At this time? What did he want?

APSARA   He wanted to talk to me. He knocked immediately after you left. I thought it was you.

PADMA   What did he want?

APSARA   I'm not sure. He's crazy.

PADMA   Tell me exactly what he said.

APSARA   He said he'll be back at nine.

PADMA   What else?

APSARA   Nothing. He just sat in silence, drank his tea, and left.

PADMA   He wants something.

APSARA   What makes you say that? Maybe he just came for a dance.

PADMA   Apsara, you're a good dancer. But you're not *that* good. Perhaps this blind man can see something we can't.

APSARA   Like what?

PADMA   A blind spot.

6.

> Night. KAMAL is seated on the swing. He is alone in the room. APSARA enters.

APSARA   I see you have a new cane.

KAMAL   It's not mine. The old man gave it to me. He told me he has no use for it anymore. He's full of mischief, that old bandit. He offered me tea this morning, hot tea, unlike the luke-warm tea you gave me. Anyway, just before I put the cup to my lips, I heard something fall into my teacup and his wife shouted, "Stop putting your dentures in the blind man's cup."

APSARA   And you prefer their tea to mine.

KAMAL   Dentures are harmless. Teeth without jaws. No malice.

APSARA   Have you got the money?

KAMAL   Ah, the money. Your neighbours are short on money.

APSARA   That's unfortunate.

KAMAL   So I found them a paying guest.

> He smiles.

APSARA   Why are you smiling?

KAMAL   Meet your new neighbour.

> Silence from APSARA.

It was an accident. Over tea, we started talking. I said, "I need to find a guesthouse nearby." He said, "Stay with us." So I said, "This is not a guesthouse," and he replied, "You are a guest and you are already in my house." At which point the old woman rushed into the room shouting, "A paying guest! My prayers have been answered. Praised be the Lord." And the old man asked, "Which Lord?" And she replied, "All three hundred of them." (pause) Anyway— where's your mother?

APSARA   In bed.

KAMAL   But it's only nine.

APSARA   She's not sleeping. She's just lying down.

KAMAL   Are we disturbing her?

APSARA   We had this place soundproofed.

KAMAL   Has she ever broken anyone's hands with an iron rod?

APSARA Once. A politician came here and tried cocaine. It was his first time. After that he was like a bull. He started touching me. She came in with an iron rod and broke both his wrists. Any more questions?

KAMAL As I explained to you this morning, we have to get to know each other.

APSARA As long as you pay.

KAMAL Payment is a problem. I can't afford to pay you. I'm quite poor.

APSARA No money, no conversation.

KAMAL But I'm a bookseller.

APSARA Then stop coming here. Do bookseller things.

KAMAL I'm not even a bookstore owner. I work on commission.

APSARA No money, no conversation.

KAMAL But these are my life savings.

APSARA You expect me to believe you're spending your life savings on dance?

KAMAL They're called life savings for a reason. You spend them on things that will save your life.

APSARA How am I going to save your life?

KAMAL We'll need all the money we have for our life together when you leave this place. So please don't make me pay you.

APSARA You have quite an imagination.

KAMAL Fine. Here's three thousand more.

But KAMAL does not move.

APSARA Where is it?

KAMAL Oh, you noticed.

He blows her a kiss.

BOMBAY BLACK / 83

The currency of love.

APSARA What a nightmare.

KAMAL Love is full of nightmares, my dear. I learnt that as a child.

APSARA How touching.

KAMAL Love is a big fat flower. Petal by petal it unfolds. Then it gets thinner and sicker, sicker and thinner, until it is just a stalk. Sharp enough to poke someone in the eyes with.

APSARA Is that what happened to you? Did someone poke you in the eyes and cause you to lose your sight?

KAMAL What beast would do such a thing?

APSARA One of your customers, perhaps. After reading the rubbish you tried to sell him.

KAMAL That's funny. It's funny that someone who should be wracked with guilt is so… so frivolous about my blindness.

APSARA Guilt? Why would I be wracked with guilt?

His tone changes.

KAMAL Because *you're* the reason I'm blind.

APSARA What?

KAMAL You took my sight away.

APSARA Have you lost your mind?

KAMAL I was ten when it happened. In the village of Vajra.

APSARA Vajra? But that's where…

KAMAL You're from. Your mother's name is Padma. Your father's name is Vishnu. He's a priest.

APSARA Look—who are you?

KAMAL I am ten years old. You are three. You're walking around a fire. There's smoke in your eyes. You're crying out for your mother.

APSARA How do you know that?

KAMAL I was there.

APSARA That's a dream I've had since I was little.

KAMAL A dream? So you've converted our life into a dream. That's okay with me. The crackling of wood can be heard even in dreams. It starts slowly at first... faint... as though it isn't really there...

> *The sound of a fire. Slowly, whatever KAMAL describes comes to life before them.*

You're three years old and you're dressed in yellow. Same colour as the fire almost. You're circling around the fire and its smoke is making your eyes water. But there are also tears. The sound of the priest chanting. You're scared and so am I. Oh yes, I'm right there with you. I'm ten years old. I'm scared too, and as we circle the fire I look at you, a sorry three-year-old girl, crying for her mother, begging her to take you away. And I'm ashamed of myself. Even though it's not my fault, I feel responsible for making you scared. And all those people. Those stupid, stupid villagers with grins on their faces as though we were in a circus, you and I, two little monkeys getting married. That's what it felt like. We were monkeys forced to walk round a fire by our parents. And then I did it. I touched you. I held your hand out of pity because you were more scared than I. And the moment I did that, a blinding flash of light, like a rod of lightning had pierced my eyes, as though my pupils had committed some horrible crime and needed to be punished. And then it was I who was screaming for my mother. I should have run into the flames, Apsara. I'm sorry that I ran the other way, into the crowd. Into that dumb, sweaty, brain-fucked crowd. *(pause)* So let me ask you now: Do you know who I am?

> *She is nervous. She gets up. He senses this.*

Don't try to leave.

> *He moves towards her.*

You took my sight. Now I want it back.

She tries to move away from him, but he senses where she is. He is like a predator now waiting to pounce on her. She is extremely still, aware that he can sense the slightest movement.

Your touch made me blind all those years ago. If I touch you again, I will see. That's why I'm here. I want you to hold my hand, Apsara. Give me my sight back.

He extends his arm to her. She does not take it.

Don't make me force you.

She makes a run for it. He grabs her hand.

I want my sight back!

A blinding flash of light on APSARA. Then lights fade almost to black.

APSARA I... I can't see. I can't see a thing. Why can't I see?

KAMAL My name is Kamal. Whatever I have told you is true. Does my name sound familiar now?

APSARA No. Kamal. No.

KAMAL Don't just say my name like that. Say it like it means something. Do you know what my name means?

APSARA Lotus.

KAMAL Is that how you treat a lotus? Like a piece of dog shit? As though it is not white and pure? A lotus floats on water like a king. Know that and then say my name. *(pause)* Say it.

APSARA Kamal.

KAMAL Again.

APSARA Kamal.

KAMAL You're scared, aren't you?

APSARA What have you done to me?

KAMAL I touched you, just like I did at our wedding. That's all.

APSARA Why can't I see?

KAMAL   I don't know. *(pause)* I asked if you're scared.

APSARA   Yes.

KAMAL   So was I, Apsara. I was terrified when it happened to me all those years ago. All I did was touch you. And I went blind. Just like that.

APSARA   I don't remember any of this. I swear.

KAMAL   There's only one thing you need to remember. You were three. I was ten. I, my dear, am your husband.

7.

> *APSARA is moving in the darkness like a scared animal. PADMA enters. Turns the light on.*

PADMA   What did he want? What did you find out about the blind man?

APSARA   Is the light on or off?

PADMA   Light? What light?

APSARA   The light in this room. Is it on or off?

PADMA   What sort of idiot talk is that?

APSARA   Just answer the question. Please.

PADMA   It's on. Apsara, are you okay?

> *APSARA shakes her head.*

What's wrong?

APSARA   I can't see.

PADMA   You can't see what?

APSARA   I can't see anything. Not the walls, the swing, nothing.

PADMA   Are you playing a game with me?

APSARA   Yes, this is a game. It has to be. *(pause)* When was the first time I dreamt about the fire?

PADMA What difference?

APSARA Just tell me.

PADMA You must have been four or five.

APSARA Are you sure?

PADMA I remember it clearly. You came crying to me in the middle of the night. You said that you dreamt you were around a fire and there was smoke in your eyes.

APSARA Then what happened?

PADMA Nothing. I held you in my arms and put you back to sleep.

APSARA Is that all you did?

PADMA I whispered in your ear, "It's only a dream. Go to sleep. It's only a dream."

APSARA Who is Kamal?

No response from PADMA.

Tell me about Kamal.

PADMA I don't know any Kamal. What's wrong with you?

APSARA I'm terrified, mother.

PADMA Of what?

APSARA My husband.

PADMA What? But there is no...

PADMA reaches to comfort APSARA. APSARA recoils the moment PADMA touches her. PADMA exits.

8.

Later. The same night. There is a knock on the door. The knocking continues. APSARA slowly finds her way to the door in the darkness. But does not open it.

KAMAL   Apsara, it's Kamal. Open the door. *(pause)* I want to know if you're okay. Let me in.

APSARA   What did you do to me?

KAMAL   I touched you, just like I did at our wedding. That's all I did.

APSARA   Why can't I see?

KAMAL   I don't know. But if you let me in, we can help each other.

APSARA   I want you to leave.

KAMAL   If that's what you want, then I will walk away this instant. But understand that every single day, when you wake up from your sleep, you will realize you are blind. From this moment on, you will live in one colour—black. And it will be the colour of absolute terror. You'll have to learn everything all over again. How to walk. How many steps to take to go to the toilet. Each and every sound will haunt you. To this day, I feel there are snakes at my feet. In the village, on my way to school, the children would shout, "Snake, snake," and I'd freeze in terror, until I heard their laughter. Blindness is not the absence of light, but the sheer presence of darkness. It's like a switch has been turned off, and it might never come back on again.

APSARA   What do you want from me?

She opens the door.

What do you want? You've got your revenge.

KAMAL   Revenge? You think I'm here for revenge?

APSARA   Then what do you call taking my sight away?

He enters.

KAMAL   Love. A mad love. A love so strong we could uproot trees with it.

She walks away from him and sits on the swing.

APSARA   I don't love you.

KAMAL Not now, maybe. But in a day or two, who knows? In a day or two we could be lovers. You are an Apsara. I am a lotus. We are bound together.

APSARA What do you mean?

KAMAL The very first Apsara lived in a lake with a single lotus. The two were inseparable.

APSARA I am not a celestial nymph in heaven. And you are not a flower. We are in Bombay and there's shit on the road and it costs only a few hundred rupees to have someone murdered.

KAMAL That might be true, but let us not forget what the name means. "The Good Bay." That's what the Portuguese called this city. So good things can happen here too, if you believe. Let us believe that I am indeed a lotus. The only time the lotus withered was when the Apsara left the lake on a mission.

APSARA And what mission would that be?

KAMAL Do you not know the story of the first Apsara?

APSARA I don't like stories.

KAMAL Centuries ago, when heaven existed, it had many gods. There was Brahma the Creator, Shiva the Destroyer, Krishna the Lover…

APSARA Were there no goddesses?

KAMAL Not yet. So at the end of the day, when these male gods were done creating mountains, rivers, and gardens, when they were done designing planets and answering people's prayers, they sat in heaven's court and someone suggested, "How about some dance?" All the gods loved the suggestion, so they created this beautiful woman: round hips, big black eyes, long hair. The world's first Apsara. She danced for them and all the gods were mesmerized.

APSARA They became like vegetables. Each and every god wanted Apsara to himself.

KAMAL So you do know the story.

APSARA   No, but I know men.

KAMAL   The gods started using their powers against each other. Shiva released cobras from his matted hair and choked Brahma's throat. Krishna transformed his flute into a spear and hurled it at Shiva. Suddenly the gods realized what they were doing.

APSARA   Fighting over a woman. A mere dancer. The shame of it.

KAMAL   They were so enraged that they banished Apsara to a lake. The lake contained a single lotus. The Apsara and the lotus fell in love. But that love was not enough. The Apsara left the lake to seek revenge on the gods. The moment she left, the lotus started to wither.

APSARA   Did she get her revenge?

KAMAL   She secretly went to each god and professed her love. She danced for the god, sucked up all his energy, and killed him. Until there were no gods left.

APSARA   So what's the moral?

KAMAL   I find questions more interesting than morals.

APSARA   What's the question?

KAMAL   On whom does *this* Apsara want to take revenge?

APSARA   No one.

KAMAL   In good time you will tell me. In good time. But know this. A lotus cannot survive without an Apsara. That's why I'm here. I need you so that I may live.

APSARA   Mythology is the poor man's diet.

KAMAL   The rich can afford to be realistic. (*pause*) Come with me, my Apsara.

APSARA   I'm not going anywhere. I want my sight back. What's happened to me?

KAMAL   I don't know. (*pause*) Can you hear that?

APSARA   No, what is it?

KAMAL It's a horse carriage. All the lovers of Bombay go for rides on them.

APSARA I don't like lovers.

KAMAL Listen.

APSARA I can't hear a thing.

KAMAL The blind pluck things out of thin air. That's how we live. Darkness is a blank slate. Draw what you want on it. Listen. Listen to that carriage.

The sound of the carriage.

Hear its wheels spinning, grinding against the uneven road. It's coming closer. Now smell the *beedi* that the old man smokes as he rides his carriage. There is also the fragrance of *champa* that are on the floor of the carriage. Take it all in. Now feel the horses. Touch the sweat on their backs. See their skin shining under the streetlights. Can you see them? They're black. The horses are pure black. Smell them. Smell the shit they leave on the road below. Don't be afraid to smell the shit. The carriage is very close. Are you ready? We'll jump on the count of three.

The sound of the carriage gets louder.

One-two-three.

He sits on the swing. It becomes the carriage.

Sorry, excuse us. The old man looks a bit concerned. Ignore him. Look at the Gateway of India instead.

APSARA is silent.

Describe it to me.

APSARA It's brownish yellow. It has four turrets and a central dome.

KAMAL What else? Describe the scene to me.

APSARA is silent.

What do you see?

APSARA Photographers.

KAMAL Photographers?

APSARA Yes, amateur photographers who take photos of the tourists beside the Gateway for a few rupees.

KAMAL What else?

APSARA There's a *chaiwala* with a small kerosene stove selling tea in paper cups. There are stray dogs playing, there are workers asleep on the ground, and there's a security guard keeping people away from the Gateway.

KAMAL Now we're standing right under the dome. I can feel the heat of lights all over my body. Do you notice anything unusual about the Gateway?

APSARA No, nothing unusual.

KAMAL The Gateway of India is now moving off the ground and sliding into the water. Quietly. Like a stranger sneaking into someone else's pool. It's floating on water, Apsara, and no one's on it but us. We will let it take us far out to sea. Now everyone from the Taj Mahal Hotel behind us is looking in astonishment. All those foreigners who stay at the Taj are calling their loved ones in London, New York and Paris, "Bombay is demented. Buildings float on water." And their relatives abroad are replying, "Stop smoking that Bombay Black, mother! It's all that Bombay Black!" *(pause)* We must be careful we don't collide into any ships. We just passed the Vikrant. Now we're approaching the Sea Princess. Now we're past the huge ships. We're so deep into the Arabian Sea even the fish don't wander here. So here we are, you and I, not a soul around, only the sound of the waves and the whisper of the wind to keep us company. Let's talk.

> *They stand in the middle of the Arabian Sea. They listen to the wind and the waves.*

APSARA It's not possible. It's just not possible.

KAMAL What.

APSARA That two people can blind each other by mere touch.

KAMAL   The universe is a complete bastard.

>   *They sit in silence in the middle of the Arabian Sea.*

So tell me, is it just you and your mother? Or does someone else live with you?

APSARA   Just us.

KAMAL   What about your father?

APSARA   We don't know where he is.

KAMAL   How long has it been since you saw him?

APSARA   Ten years. *(pause)* Why are you asking me about my father?

KAMAL   Because he's dying.

APSARA   What?

KAMAL   Your father doesn't have much time left.

APSARA   You know him?

KAMAL   He was the priest at our wedding. In order to find you, I had to start with him. I promised him that if I ever found you, I'd tell him. He wants to see you.

>   *Silence.*

He's dying. He wants to see you before he dies.

APSARA   What illness does he have?

KAMAL   He hasn't been to a doctor. He doesn't believe in them.

APSARA   Does he know where we are?

KAMAL   I haven't told him.

APSARA   Are you sure?

KAMAL   Yes, I'm sure. Why don't you want him to know?

APSARA   Where is he? The last we heard he had left the village.

KAMAL   He's in Bombay. Do you want to see him?

APSARA   No. *(pause)* No.

KAMAL But the man's dying.

APSARA Look—what the hell do you want from me? You've already taken my sight. What else do you want?

KAMAL An exchange took place, Apsara. All those years ago, when you were three and I was ten, an exchange took place.

APSARA An exchange of what?

KAMAL An exchange of sight. I don't believe our sight has been lost forever. I think it's been banished to make way for something greater.

APSARA Like what?

KAMAL I don't know. All I know is that there's all this water around us. We're two blind people in the middle of the Arabian Sea. That's all I know. *(pause)* Step into the water with me. An Apsara belongs in the water with the lotus.

He steps into the water. She does not. He senses this.

No one can see us now. All the tourists are asleep. The fish are too deep. The drug smugglers and their small boats are nowhere to be found. I don't know how this is going to turn out. Come with me. Right now, all I have to offer is the water.

9.

APSARA alone in the room. She is trying to find the door that leads to the inner room. Enter PADMA.

PADMA What are you doing?

No answer.

Apsara, what are you doing?

APSARA Help me pack my things.

PADMA What for?

APSARA We must leave. We must leave Bombay.

PADMA Apsara, calm down. We'll go to a doctor. There must be something wrong with the nerves that connect the brain and the eyes. The body is a strange beast. Who knows what angers it.

APSARA We must leave before he finds us.

PADMA Who?

APSARA My father.

> *PADMA stands still.*

Kamal met my father.

PADMA Are you sure?

APSARA In order to find me, Kamal started with him.

PADMA He's alive... the bastard's alive...

APSARA He's dying.

PADMA Of what?

APSARA I don't know. Kamal said he's very sick. *(pause)* My father wants to see me. We must leave at once.

PADMA He wants to see you.

> *APSARA extends her arm for help.*

APSARA Where are you?

> *PADMA sits on the swing.*

PADMA I'm here. On the swing. Come here.

> *APSARA finds her way to the swing. PADMA holds APSARA's hand, makes her sit.*

APSARA We must move to another city.

PADMA We can't keep running from him.

APSARA We have to.

> *Pause.*

PADMA What if you were to see him again?

APSARA I can't.

PADMA But suppose you have to.

APSARA Why would I have to?

PADMA Let him find us.

APSARA What?

PADMA It might be your purpose.

APSARA My purpose? What the hell are you talking about?

PADMA Let me rephrase it. What if it's your *function*—leading your father here. To *me*.

APSARA To you?

PADMA You know, when you use a piece of meat. *(pause)* There was this hunter once. And he was tired and hungry and wounded. A hyena had wounded him and now he was alone in the forest... tired and hungry... and if he did not eat, he'd die... so he cut off a piece of his own flesh, from his thigh, and left it on the ground and hid. The hyena came for that flesh and it was too distracted to see the hunter... and so the hunter got his chance—he killed the hyena.

APSARA What are you saying?

PADMA I'm saying that I'm tired and hungry... and...

> *APSARA moves away.*

APSARA You're out of your mind.

PADMA And it's a beautiful, magical feeling.

APSARA But what about me?

PADMA What about you?

APSARA I never want to see him again. You promised.

PADMA You'll have to.

> *She caresses APSARA.*

Apsara, in order to survive, I will sacrifice my own flesh.

APSARA gets off the swing.

Where are you going? I need you more than ever, my dear.

APSARA What is wrong with you?

PADMA Nothing. I'm finally telling you the truth.

APSARA tries to find her way to the inner room.

APSARA I'm leaving. I…

PADMA Oh? And where will you go—to a school for the blind? You can't leave. You obviously weren't listening.

PADMA gets off the swing.

There was a hunter.

She moves towards APSARA.

There was a hyena.

PADMA pushes APSARA. She falls to the floor.

There was a piece of flesh.

PADMA walks away. APSARA alone on stage.

END OF ACT ONE

ACT TWO

1.

APSARA alone on stage. She has her anklets on. She walks the length and breadth of the room. She touches everything in the room, tries to feel the darkness. She starts moving, dancing. She does so gracefully to the sounds around her. The sound of fire interrupts her dance. The sound of chanting, her father's prayers at the wedding, the same sounds of her dream begin to haunt her. She continues to dance, but is no longer graceful. It is a dance of resistance. Now temple bells distort her world, disturb her. She tries to continue with the dance but is defeated by the temple bells. Enter PADMA. APSARA senses her presence.

APSARA   Why didn't you tell me I was married to Kamal?

PADMA   What good would it have done?

APSARA   Whose idea was it?

PADMA   Idea? It's been going on since hundreds of years. To protect the girl child from being raped by sultans and warlords and whatnot, parents married off their infants when they were in their cradles. So don't worry—historically, you were well past the marriageable age. Kamal's family asked for you because your father was the most respected priest in the village. And Kamal's family owned land. The alliance made sense.

APSARA   Made sense? I was three.

PADMA   We had found a good match. There were two baby girls in the village who were drowned in tubs of milk simply because they were girls. But we kept you. So be grateful.

APSARA   What exactly happened that day?

PADMA   The moment Kamal touched you he went blind.

APSARA   How?

PADMA Who knows? Perhaps it's nature's way of proving that it's more powerful than man. You were doomed right from the start, Apsara. A boy went blind the moment he touched you. The villagers wanted your blood. They started shouting that you were cursed, that you were a dangerous child. So your father announced there and then that if you were to devote your life to the temple, it would appease the gods and it would prevent anyone else from getting hurt. That was the only way to calm the villagers down, those hungry, bloodsucking fools.

APSARA And you let father take me away?

PADMA I objected. I refused to let you go. He said that if we offered you to the temple, the gods would offer us a boon. I would be granted a son. He was the head priest of the village, a learned man. I believed him.

APSARA You sacrificed one child so you could have another.

PADMA The universe plays us. We are pawns. We always sacrifice ourselves for something greater.

APSARA A son is greater.

PADMA A son will always be greater. It was a matter of face. How could I stand before my family and say, "My only contribution to this world is a *girl?*"

APSARA But the son never came. That brother of mine was never born. What happened, mother? Did you not appease the gods enough?

PADMA Don't worry about the gods for now. Just make sure you appease *me*. Ask Kamal to bring your father here.

APSARA I can't.

PADMA Don't make this difficult.

APSARA I won't do it.

PADMA I see. Stay here. I'll be right back.

APSARA Where are you going?

PADMA To get some meat.

She exits and returns with a large chunk of red meat.
She puts it under APSARA's nose.

Smell this. .

She thrusts it into APSARA's hand.

Squash it. Feel it between your fingers. Soon, your father will feel like that. Soft and dead.

APSARA tries to break away from her grip. But PADMA is strong. She takes APSARA to the window.

APSARA Where are you taking me?

PADMA To feed the eagles. It's a little early for them, but we'll wait. Now I'm asking you again: Will you make Kamal bring your father to me?

APSARA No.

PADMA I see an eagle. It's far away, but it's coming.

APSARA I don't like this. Please.

PADMA Look at it. Those powerful wings. Now that's a *man.* If only I could have those wings over me for just one night. What a man an eagle is. A protector. A god. It's spotted us. Your eyes are of no use to you now, are they?

APSARA Mother, please...

PADMA Will you bring your father to me?

APSARA He's dying. Let him go.

PADMA He shall die by *my* hand. You will help me.

APSARA I can't see him again. Please.

PADMA Listen. Listen to that sound.

The frenzied sound of eagles, frighteningly loud and close. PADMA presses the meat against APSARA's face.

You will help me.

APSARA I will...

She lets go of APSARA.

PADMA   *(to eagles)* Come my children. Come to Padma.

2.

Afternoon. KAMAL and APSARA are together. They sit in silence for a while.

KAMAL   There are two kinds of silences. The first is a peaceful one. But the silence I hear right now, the silence that comes from you, is a loud, screaming silence.

APSARA does not respond.

The kind of silence that comes when the past haunts you.

APSARA is still quiet.

You should have stepped into the water with me.

APSARA   What difference does it make?

KAMAL   We belong in the water. Together.

APSARA   Stories don't decide where I belong. I do.

KAMAL   By rejecting the water, you have chosen something else.

APSARA   What's that?

KAMAL   Revenge. The Apsara told the lotus that she could not truly love until she had taken revenge. The lotus begged her to stay, but the Apsara did not listen. When the Apsara returned to the lake after vanquishing the gods, she looked for the lotus. She was crushed to find the lotus withered and dead on the surface of the water. She spent the rest of her days staring at her reflection in the water until she grew old, until she could no longer tell the difference between the ripples in the water and the lines on her face. Had she chosen water, things would have turned out differently.

APSARA   What would have happened?

KAMAL   We'll find out only if you join me.

APSARA I don't understand you. How can you live in a story after spending so many years without sight?

KAMAL If a snake bites you, what will you do? Will you spend your time chasing the snake, or ensuring that the poison does not paralyze you?

APSARA Once the poison enters your bloodstream it stays there forever.

KAMAL Tell me what happened with your father.

APSARA This has nothing to do with my father.

KAMAL The Apsara is staying out of the water for a reason. She wants revenge.

APSARA Why do you care?

KAMAL We must know everything about each other. That's the only way for us to find a way to… to *solve* this.

APSARA You think there's a chance that I can get my sight back?

KAMAL There's always a chance. Tell me what happened with your father.

>   *Pause.*

APSARA Tell me to dance.

KAMAL Dance.

APSARA Command me to dance for you.

KAMAL Dance for me, Apsara.

>   *They are in the temple. She dances. At first, the dance is innocent. It is the dance of a girl.*

APSARA Now let the force of your words turn a child into a woman.

KAMAL Dance for me.

APSARA Say it as if every bit of flesh in your body is reaching for me.

KAMAL Dance.

> *The dance becomes seductive.*

APSARA Yes, father. You are the most respected priest in the village. I am seven years old. Maybe eight.

> *She moves towards KAMAL. She holds him, lies on the floor, lowers him as well. She makes him lie on top of her. She spreads her legs.*

KAMAL I can't do this...

> *KAMAL tries to get off her. APSARA holds him by the hair and prevents him from getting off her.*

APSARA You said we must know everything about each other.

KAMAL I can't...

> *She pulls his mouth close to hers. She is trembling, her voice quivers.*

APSARA I ask my father what he is doing. He tells me not to worry. He tells me to close my eyes. I am seven years old. Maybe eight. I look at my father's face and his eyes are closed. He starts making sounds. His mouth smells of country liquor. So I turn my face away from him and stare at the white floor of the temple... and I feel my father's amulet against my cheek, the cold steel of his amulet... as he rocks back and forth... back and forth... and whispers into my ear, "I love you, Apsara... I love you..."

...and my father opens his eyes... he is pleased with me... he is full of sweat and he strokes my head, "You are the only thing I can ever love, Apsara... you are the only thing I love..."

> *KAMAL finally breaks away. He kneels towards her.*

KAMAL I'm sorry. I had no idea.

APSARA Will you help me kill him?

KAMAL What?

APSARA You were right. I want revenge. I want you to help me kill him.

KAMAL I'm not a murderer. The lotus had no part in the revenge.

APSARA That's why the two didn't last. What if the lotus had helped the Apsara to seek revenge? Maybe the lotus would have survived. *(pause)* You won't have to lay a finger on him.

KAMAL I won't allow you to kill.

APSARA My mother will do it.

KAMAL You speak of this as though you are killing a goat or chicken.

APSARA So you think he deserves to live.

KAMAL No, I... what good will it do?

APSARA All you need to do is lead him to us. Tell him I want to see him. Tell him I live alone. That my mother and I are separated.

KAMAL I won't lead a man to his death.

APSARA You said you loved me.

KAMAL But this is madness.

APSARA You said it was a mad love.

KAMAL This is not a game.

APSARA Of course it is. "Close your eyes, Apsara. Don't tell mother otherwise I will kill her." Trust me. It's a game. Will you do it? *(pause)* You prefer to tend to the poison. I prefer to kill the snake.

KAMAL How can you bear to see him again?

APSARA I see him every single day. I can feel that cold steel amulet of his every single day. But if his flesh leaves the earth, perhaps it will leave me too.

KAMAL I'm sorry. I don't think I can do it.

He walks away.

APSARA Where are you going?

KAMAL I... I don't know.

APSARA Sit down. We're not done yet.

KAMAL We're done.

APSARA I'm sorry for what I did to you.

KAMAL It's not your fault.

APSARA The thing about the snake. Where the children scared you on your way to school. Did that really happen?

KAMAL Yes. After a while, I stopped getting scared. That's when they would spit on me and ask me to guess whose spit it was. Finally, my parents and I had to leave the village.

APSARA You said an exchange took place. "An exchange of sight." Those were your exact words. What did you mean by that?

KAMAL I don't believe that my sight is lost. I came here expecting to get my sight back when I touched you. I did not come here to make you blind.

APSARA You're right. You came here to bring me my father.

3.

PADMA and APSARA on the swing.

PADMA Did he agree?

APSARA No.

PADMA Why not?

APSARA He's too soft.

PADMA Then make him hard.

APSARA This is *your* little fantasy, mother.

PADMA My dear daughter. This is about killing the man who raped you at the age of eight.

APSARA Seven. Not eight. If you're going to kill him, get the facts straight.

PADMA When your father called us whores and banished us from the village, he was right about one of us.

APSARA You could have fought him.

PADMA I did. He accused me of selling you for money. Everyone believed him. My own family spat on me. The entire village spat on us. Do you not remember? Or did you think their spit was nourishing rain? Perhaps you deserve to be spat on.

APSARA Yes. All those days when I shivered under his body, as he kept whispering that he would kill *you* if I told a soul... yes, I deserve to be spat on.

PADMA You were a beautiful, horrible child. I saw how he looked at you. I saw the way his eyes moved.

APSARA You knew. You knew he wanted me and you created a little paradise for him.

PADMA What wife does not look the other way? What wife can bear to see that the man she loves, the man she gave her heart to, is happier with a... with a child! It's what women do. We're taught to look the other way.

APSARA It was your idea to send me to the temple.

PADMA I told you. It was your father's. After the wedding, the villagers saw you as a threat. As something demonic.

APSARA I understand.

PADMA What do you understand?

APSARA I was his universe. I understand how you feel, mother. It's one thing to be abused. But to be humiliated and completely unloved... perhaps that's more painful.

APSARA smiles.

Yes, that is more painful...

PADMA Tell me, in all these years, have I ever forced you to live with me?

> *APSARA stays silent.*

Answer my question.

APSARA No.

PADMA Have I ever stopped you from leaving?

APSARA No.

PADMA Then why do you choose to live with me?

APSARA I need you to put food in my mouth.

PADMA On the contrary, I need you. Dance is your gift. Not mine. You could go and dance in any one of Bombay's bars. Bar girls make lots of money. Tell me the real reason you continue to stay by my side.

APSARA That *is* the real reason.

PADMA No, my dear. The truth is, you are just as unloved as I am. You hope that by staying with me, someday we can put the past behind us and we'll have a normal mother-daughter relationship. You know, we'll have our quarrels, but we'll also chit-chat, watch movies, go for walks. But more than anything, you are looking for me to tell you that the pain you feel will go away. You want some *solution* to that pain. Now I'm giving it to you.

Picture this, my love: Your father will come to meet his beloved. The two of you will sit on this swing and talk. There will come a point when he will rest his head on your shoulders and you will comfort him, breathe into his ear like you did when he was on top of you. You will stroke his back, his smooth lizard's back, and you will think of the time you lay under him, trembling, your head turned to the side like a corpse, and that is when I will walk up to him, tap him on the back, look him in the eye and…

> *She moves towards the exit.*

APSARA Where are you going?

PADMA   To fetch Kamal.

APSARA   He won't do it. He's not a killer.

PADMA   My dear piece of meat, everyone's a killer. It's just a matter of incentive.

4.

> *PADMA enters the room. This time she helps KAMAL walk.*

KAMAL   You're helping me find my way this time.

PADMA   You scratch my back… or I'll scratch your eyes out.

KAMAL   There's not much you can do to me that life hasn't already.

PADMA   It's dangerous to think that way, my friend.

KAMAL   I am not your friend.

PADMA   Have a seat.

KAMAL   I'll stand.

PADMA   I'll keep it simple then. There is something I want from you.

KAMAL   I know.

PADMA   There is something you want from me.

KAMAL   I want nothing from you.

PADMA   You want Apsara.

KAMAL   Apsara is not yours.

PADMA   The problem with you is that you rely too much on sound. The most important things are unspoken.

KAMAL   Enlighten me.

PADMA   Hate makes for much stronger glue than love. Apsara and I are connected with a beautiful, common hatred. A bond that will last a lifetime.

KAMAL She can choose to leave you.

PADMA It's been ten years since she saw her father. But he is by her side every second. It's the same with me. You can take her with you. But you will never have her. Only I can give her to you.

KAMAL I'm listening.

PADMA Bring my husband to me. And you shall have Apsara. After all, she does love you.

KAMAL She said that?

PADMA Not at all. But in all these years, she's never spoken to a man. Even the smell of a man makes her ill. She is at ease with you and it frightens her. She is afraid that you are a man who might be *good* for her. All she needs is for me to tell her that she can love. That she can *be* loved.

KAMAL And you will do that?

PADMA If you bring my husband to me.

KAMAL There's no guarantee that she will go with me. She might still choose to stay with you.

PADMA Not if I don't give her that choice.

KAMAL What do you mean?

PADMA I have no use for Apsara once my husband is gone. The only reason I kept her was because I knew he would come back for her. Once he is gone, I will go too.

KAMAL What will you do?

PADMA I don't know. I'll go back to my village. Watch children fly kites. Grow vegetables. And then one day, as I'm plucking my beloved tomatoes and carrots, I'll slice my throat. Or maybe I won't. In a way, my future is in your hands. Can you bring yourself to kill a child-fucker in order to gain Apsara?

KAMAL I think I can.

PADMA Don't think.

KAMAL   I can. I will.

PADMA   Then I shall give you your wife back.

KAMAL   I'd like to speak to her before I leave.

PADMA   I'm not done yet. I'd like to know about my husband. I need to form a fresh picture of him in my mind. It's been ten years. Would you mind answering a few questions?

KAMAL   Go ahead.

PADMA   What does he sound like? Is his voice still rough and raspy?

KAMAL   You don't need to test me. His voice is smooth.

PADMA   Ah, yes, smooth as ever.

KAMAL   Except when he coughs.

PADMA   Is he dying of TB?

KAMAL   He wouldn't say.

PADMA   What else?

KAMAL   What would you like to know?

PADMA   Does he live alone?

KAMAL   No, he has a servant.

PADMA   Man or woman?

KAMAL   An old woman.

PADMA   I see. Did he mention Apsara to you?

KAMAL   Yes. I told him I was looking for her. He said he didn't know where she was. He said that if I ever found her, I should let him know.

PADMA   What else did he say about her?

KAMAL   That he would like to see her before he dies.

PADMA   Did he say why?

KAMAL He wants to be at peace. He said she is the only thing he ever loved.

PADMA Is that what he said?

KAMAL Yes.

PADMA Tell me his exact words.

KAMAL I just did.

PADMA Word for word. Say it.

KAMAL "Apsara is the only thing I ever loved." That's what he said.

PADMA Again.

KAMAL "Apsara is the only thing I ever loved."

PADMA Again.

KAMAL "Apsara is the only thing I ever loved."

PADMA One last time.

> *She exits.*

KAMAL "Apsara is the only thing I ever loved."

> *APSARA enters.*

Apsara?

APSARA Yes.

KAMAL Before I fetch your father, I want you to be sure.

APSARA What did my mother tell you to make you agree?

KAMAL I just want you to be sure that you want him dead. Think hard. This is not something we can ever come back from.

APSARA When I remember the first time I saw his cock, I want him dead. When I think of my mother and the fact that she knew what he was doing to me, I want *her* dead. The rest of the time I feel numb. It's like trying to decide if I should raise my right hand or my left hand to scratch an itch. Does it matter?

KAMAL Is the itch really there?

APSARA It's there. The itch is there.

KAMAL Do you remember the first time you saw me?

APSARA I told you I have no memory of us as children.

KAMAL Not then. Now.

APSARA You had the lights turned off.

KAMAL I want you to take a good look at yourself.

APSARA I know what I look like. I have mirrors.

KAMAL A mirror is the last thing we should look at ourselves in. A reflection is a *likeness* of the self. It means we only see the things about ourselves that we like. We must use our hands. The lines on your hands correspond to the lines on your face. When you move your hands against your face, the lines fit in. The parts that don't are the parts that are wrong with you. Why is it that whenever we are in grief or shock, we put our face in our hands? Because new lines have appeared and we are trying to make sense of them. But the lines that *fit* will lead you to what's good for you. Trust me. Hold your face in your hands.

>   *Slowly she does.*

Now glide your palms across your face. Very slowly. Your hands will fit in. As though the lines are grooves.

>   *She tries but nothing happens.*

APSARA I don't feel anything.

KAMAL You're going too fast. Think of your face as a vault. And you have to listen to the clicks to get the combination.

>   *She does. Her hand clicks in.*

Do you feel anything?

APSARA Yes.

KAMAL Now pick a line on your face. Pick a line that fits really well into your hand. Can you find one?

APSARA Yes.

KAMAL Now follow it. Let it lead you.

APSARA I'm moving very fast. As though my brain is travelling at great speed along a thin railway track.

KAMAL Follow it to the end of the line.

APSARA I've stopped.

KAMAL Where are you?

APSARA I'm by a lake. It's very sunny. I know this place. I used to sit there alone when I was little. My mother used to meet me there. She used to bring me food because I was never allowed into the village. I used to sit there and imagine myself dancing on the water's surface. It's been ten years since I last saw the lake. I'm moving again. Slower this time. There's a row of coconut trees and a well.

KAMAL Look around you.

APSARA There's a small group of thatched houses. An old man is selling bananas from his small shop. The bananas hang like yellow garlands in front of him.

KAMAL What else?

APSARA I'm walking with my father. We stop outside the banana shop and I buy bananas from the old man. That's me, I'm three years old. I see a young boy appear from behind the banana shop. He's looking at me… but I don't know who he is. He's looking at me very closely.

KAMAL Is he dressed in blue?

APSARA Yes. How did you know that?

KAMAL That boy is me. That was the first time I saw you. I was taking a look at my future bride.

APSARA You're crying.

KAMAL   I was scared. I was ten years old and all I knew was kite flying. All I knew was how to run in the rain, and when the rain got too heavy I would use a large banana leaf to shield myself. My whole body fit under a banana leaf—that's how small I was, and I was being forced to get married. I kept looking at you and wondered what it all meant. But then I saw that you were tinier than I was. *(pause)* Take a good look at that girl. Is that a girl who can kill?

> *Pause.*

Is that a girl who can kill?

APSARA   I'm no longer that girl.

KAMAL   Come with me. We can start a new life. Darkness is a blank slate. Draw what you want on it.

APSARA   I want to draw blood.

KAMAL   If you choose revenge, the lotus will wither.

APSARA   Perhaps it's time the lotus left the water too.

> *Pause.*

KAMAL   Then I shall deliver your father to you. But before I go, I need to know something. Do I frighten you?

APSARA   All men frighten me.

KAMAL   What I mean is: Are you afraid that I might be good for you?

> *She does not answer.*

That's all I needed to know.

> *He leaves.*

5.

> *APSARA is sitting on the swing.*

PADMA   You will tell him I am dead. I died three years ago. Tell him I killed myself. That I ate rat poison. Yes, tell him that.

For a while, I'll hide and watch. I'll listen to him whisper into your ear. I've never seen him do it. I want to see what it's like. When fathers and daughters are lovers, how do they speak to each other? I want to feel the electricity in the air. I want to taste the poison in the room. Then, once I've had my fill…

She produces a butcher's knife.

…I will plunge a knife into his stomach. Let the knife remain there for a while. I'll watch him convulse. I'll look into his eyes, I'll comfort him. I'll place his head in my lap. Let him die in his wife's lap like a bleeding vegetable, as every husband should.

She places the knife in APSARA's hands.

Feel that. Feel its thickness. It's length.

APSARA Where did you get this?

PADMA I told you the butcher was a friend of mine. A dear, dear friend.

APSARA holds the knife.

Feel that blade. It's enough to make you believe in love again.

APSARA What if Kamal doesn't come?

PADMA That's not an option.

PADMA takes the knife back.

APSARA But it's been three days since he left.

PADMA He'll be here.

APSARA But let's just say that he doesn't show up.

PADMA The eagles will be devastated.

APSARA The eagles?

PADMA Why do you think I've been feeding them meat all these years? I'm going to cut your father up into little pieces and feed him to the eagles. In this city, the undertaker comes flying right to your window and you don't even need a coffin. Isn't Bombay beautiful?

APSARA   Yes. The Good Bay…

PADMA   I envy you, Apsara. You're a lucky girl. Your rage can be channelled to your father because of something that was done to *you*. My rage is empty. I'm angry about what he did to someone else.

APSARA   It's not my fault, mother. It never was.

PADMA   I don't know. At times, I feel you're right. I want to wake up just one morning, just one single morning, and feel no rage. I want to look at the sea and feel like I belong to it. That it moves for me, at least one small ripple exists for me. But how can I be at peace when I don't know whom to blame?

APSARA   It burns you, doesn't it? You can't understand why I don't want my father dead.

PADMA   What I love about you, dear child, is that you cannot decide who you want dead *more*. Me or him.

APSARA   What did you tell him?

PADMA   Who?

APSARA   Kamal. What did you say to change his mind?

PADMA   Nothing.

APSARA   I want to know.

PADMA   It might change the way you feel about him.

APSARA   I don't feel anything for him.

PADMA   Then why do you need to know?

APSARA   Tell me what you said.

PADMA   Money. If he brings your father to me, he gets lots of money.

APSARA   I don't believe you.

PADMA He's a poor bookseller. Money is more useful to him than a blind wife.

APSARA Kamal doesn't think that way.

PADMA You're right. Forget about it. Perhaps I made the whole thing up. You're right. Kamal's not like that at all. But this blade is getting cold. It needs warm flesh. I want your father, Apsara. If I don't get your father...

APSARA He'll be here.

PADMA I hope you haven't hatched a little plan with Kamal. I don't like being double-crossed.

APSARA He'll be here.

PADMA And how can you be sure? Perhaps he will knock on the door this very moment? Hah?

> *There is a knock on the door. They both acknowledge the absurdity of the knock. A knock again.*

APSARA That's him.

PADMA *(to eagles)* The feast is about to begin.

> *She exits. KAMAL enters. He is alone. He holds an earthen pot in his hands. APSARA tries to figure out if her father is there.*

KAMAL Apsara, it's me. I've come alone.

APSARA You're not alone. He's here.

KAMAL I've come alone. Your father's not here.

APSARA But the scent of him is so strong.

KAMAL I've brought his ashes. Your father passed away two days ago.

> *APSARA does not move. She just stands still.*

Apsara?

APSARA Oh, this will kill her...

> *Enter PADMA.*

PADMA What is it?

APSARA See for yourself.

PADMA Why are you holding that pot? *(to APSARA)* Why is he holding a pot?

KAMAL It's not a pot. It's an urn.

PADMA Why are you holding an urn?

KAMAL I went back to get him. He got up from his bed with great difficulty. I helped him get dressed. We started walking towards the door to come here when he collapsed in my arms. After a few minutes he stopped breathing.

PADMA No.

KAMAL I had him cremated that very night.

PADMA But... you promised to bring him here. You promised. He promised. Why did you cremate him? We could have done something. You could have got his body here. You're lying to me.

KAMAL I'm not lying.

> *He places the urn on the ground.*

This is your husband.

> *She slowly moves towards it. She looks into the urn. She does not touch it.*

PADMA That's not him.

KAMAL It's him.

PADMA You couldn't go through with it. I knew it.

> *KAMAL reaches into his pocket and takes out an amulet.*

KAMAL Perhaps you will recognize this.

> *He hands it to PADMA.*

APSARA What is it?

KAMAL His amulet.

> *KAMAL exits.*

PADMA He never took this off. Even when he had a bath... he never took this off...

> *She looks at the ashes again.*

But he had a lizard's back. Very smooth. And his lips were quite thin, almost like a woman's. And his breath... it was full of country liquor...

> *She smells the ashes.*

This doesn't smell like him... he used to sweat a lot. This is so dry...

> *She kneels and finally puts her hand in. She picks up some ash.*

Is this what your skin felt like when you were old? Is this... is this you... tell me if it's you... come on... touch me... say something... please touch me... here...

> *She rubs the ash on her face slowly.*

Feel me... please...

> *She slowly starts smearing the ashes all over her body.*
> *She removes her knife from the folds of her sari and looks*
> *at it. She looks at the blade as though she does not know*
> *what to do with it. She looks at her ash-covered body.*
> *She contemplates stabbing the ash that is all over her.*
> *And lets out a low howl.*

6.

> *PADMA and APSARA are seated. She still has ash all*
> *over her. PADMA holds the urn.*

PADMA Years and years of treachery in a pot. That's love. A woman can love a man. But a man cannot love back. When a man says, "I love you," he means "I will cause you so much pain that your heart will eat itself." You give a man all you have. At the end of the day he will scorn you because he has cunt hair stuck between his teeth. *(pause)* I don't think you should see Kamal anymore.

APSARA Why not?

PADMA Because you care about him.

APSARA I don't.

PADMA No matter where you look, you will see your father. When you kiss Kamal, you will taste your father's tongue. His hands will be your father's. His voice will turn into your father's. I don't think you should see Kamal anymore.

APSARA I feel responsible for what's happened to him.

PADMA Responsible? *He's* the reason you're blind. It was he who touched you first. Remember that.

APSARA It was also he who went blind. He's an innocent man.

PADMA But it's impossible for him to love you.

APSARA And why is that?

PADMA Because you're not a woman. You're a piece of meat shaped by your father. At a time when most children were singing songs, playing in the village fields, you were turning rotten. You have nothing to offer.

APSARA You're scared, aren't you?

PADMA Of what?

APSARA You're scared that I may leave this place. Leave *you.*

PADMA Why would I be scared?

APSARA Because now that father's dead, you have nothing to live for. But you'll still live long, *very* long, and slowly but surely you'll catch some terrible disease, and you'll have to face it without the distractions of revenge, without a daughter upon whom you can unload your spleen. You're scared, mother, I know it. And it pleases me to no end.

PADMA I'm not scared. You never meant anything to me.

APSARA   Then hold me. Hold me, Mother.

> *APSARA walks towards PADMA. Stands very close. PADMA does not respond, so APSARA holds PADMA. PADMA moves away.*

Why can't you hold your own child?

PADMA   Because you remind me of your father.

APSARA   No. I remind you that I am yours. You love me.

PADMA   I don't.

APSARA   Then prove it. Hold me close. You shouldn't feel a thing.

> *PADMA reluctantly holds APSARA.*

You're trembling, Mother.

> *PADMA is unable to speak.*

I forgive you. I forgive you, Mother. I forgive you.

> *PADMA cannot go on. She tries to break away. APSARA holds on and does not let go.*

7.

> *APSARA is seated on the swing. KAMAL enters.*

KAMAL   I've come to say goodbye.

APSARA   I see.

KAMAL   I think you should say goodbye too.

APSARA   Goodbye.

KAMAL   Not to me. Say goodbye to this place. To your mother.

> *She does not answer.*

We can help each other. Make each other happy.

> *The shadow of PADMA looming in the background.*

APSARA   You should leave.

KAMAL I'm not leaving without you.

> *He sits.*

APSARA I can still feel my father's ashes lingering in the air. They're falling against my face. Maybe he'll never leave. I want you to leave, Kamal. I don't know how to trust you.

KAMAL Perhaps that's the very reason you lost your sight.

APSARA What do you mean?

KAMAL In the past, when you saw a man, you saw his face, his eyes, his hair, his chest, you saw your father. And it repulsed you, it made you angry. Every man looked the same through your eyes. Now that your sight is lost, perhaps you will find a man who is not your father. And you have. I know you care about me.

APSARA But can I trust you?

KAMAL For that, you'll have to look at me. Take my face in your hands. If the lines fit, I'm good for you. Look at me. That's all I ask.

> *He holds her hands. Puts them to his face. Then lets go.*

Do the lines fit, Apsara? Tell me the lines fit…

APSARA The Apsara chooses revenge.

KAMAL No…

APSARA But this time, she will need the lotus' help.

KAMAL I don't understand…

APSARA The lines fit, Kamal… the lines fit. My revenge is to leave this place.

> *The shadow of PADMA disappears.*

Are you ready to leave?

KAMAL Yes.

> *She holds KAMAL's hand. She whistles loudly. A horse carriage gallops at tremendous speed.*

APSARA On the count of three. One-two-three!

> *They jump. There is a strong wind against their face as the carriage races. The sound of the wind and the carriage is very strong. KAMAL speaks above it, jubilant.*

KAMAL So you do trust me.

APSARA I might learn to.

KAMAL There's one more thing we need to do.

APSARA What's that?

KAMAL We need to fall in love.

> *The carriage rocks heavily as it gathers even more speed.*

APSARA It might take a few years. A few hundred, perhaps.

KAMAL On land, yes. Everyone knows it's impossible to fall in love on land. Ask this old man. Even he will agree. Old man, can a man and woman fall in love on land? See? Even he turns his head to the sky and laughs.

APSARA So what do you propose?

KAMAL An Apsara and a lotus belong in the water. That's where we first met thousands of years ago. To fall in love, we must fall into the sea. Are you in the mood to do something dangerous?

APSARA Yes!

KAMAL Old man, I want you to take this carriage and dive into the sea. Oh come on, old man, help us. Throw away that cigarette and do something daring. We're about to fall in love. Shower some flowers on us, old man! Lovers need flowers! I demand some flowers!

> *The horses rear up. The carriage gallops at incredible speed. A burst of flowers from the sky. They revel in the shower of flowers.*

Take those horses over the sea wall! Make us fly, old man! Make us fly!

The carriage jumps over the sea wall. Silence. They are in the air, high up in the air. Only the sound of the wind.

We're in the sky now, Apsara. We're so high we could pluck the moon and shove it up your mother's arse. This is wonderful. The whole of Bombay will see us tonight. People in the Taj Mahal Hotel will call up London, Paris, and New York and say, "I see flying horses. The whole of Bombay has gone mad." And we will say to them, "Yes, Bombay's hole is mad indeed."

They both enjoy flying for a moment.

APSARA What will we do, Kamal? We're both blind. We have nowhere to go.

KAMAL Darkness is a blank slate. Draw what you want on it. We can do anything. We'll open a bookstore.

APSARA Then it has to be a bookstore where all those who can see turn blind the moment they enter. Then they can travel thousands of years into the past where they will see an Apsara and a lotus floating on the water.

KAMAL I love the idea. *(pause)* Can I take a look at you?

KAMAL gently touches her face.

APSARA A man and woman blind each other by touch. And they want to fall in love. How can such a thing be possible?

KAMAL I don't know.

The sound of birds flying.

APSARA Perhaps they know.

KAMAL Who?

APSARA The birds. Perhaps the birds might know how such a thing can happen.

KAMAL The birds don't know.

APSARA What makes you say that?

KAMAL They're in the air all the time.

APSARA The fish. The fish must know.

KAMAL The fish think water is air, and its surface, sky.

APSARA The trees, then. It is said that trees are wise.

KAMAL Trees know a lot. But have travelled so little.

APSARA What about the wind?

KAMAL Would the wind be so restless if it knew?

APSARA The moon then. Surely the moon must know.

KAMAL The moon, you say? But the moon has no light of its own.

APSARA The grass knew. But someone cut it.

KAMAL If the stars knew, they wouldn't shine.

APSARA And if God knew…

KAMAL …would he compose this symphony of idiots?

> *They are falling towards the water with great force.*
> *They plunge into the sea. The sound of waves crashing*
> *against each other. They pop back up again.*

I can see that it's going to be very easy.

APSARA What is?

KAMAL Falling in love with you. Then having you crush my heart to bits.

APSARA Ever so gently I will step on your red thumping heart and all that love will ooze like blood, and my mouth will water because that's what I was born to do.

END OF PLAY

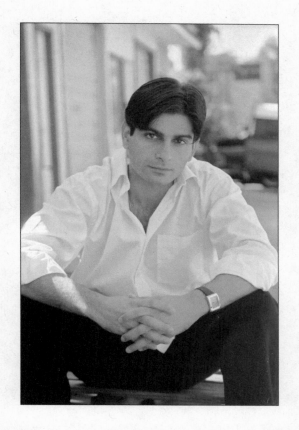

ANOSH IRANI was born and brought up in Bombay, India. He moved to Vancouver in 1998. His first play, *The Matka King*, premiered at the Arts Club Theatre Company, Vancouver, in October 2003. *Bombay Black*, commissioned by Nightswimming, was produced in January 2006 by Cahoots Theatre Projects and was the winner of 4 Dora Mavor Moore Awards including Outstanding New Play. His first novel, *The Cripple and His Talismans*, was published by Raincoast Books in 2004, and in the US and Germany in 2005. His second novel, *The Song of Kahunsha*, was published in 2006 by Doubleday Canada. Rights have been sold to the US, Italy, France, Spain, Greece, Israel, and Portugal. He is working on a new play, *My Granny the Goldfish*, for the Canadian Stage Company.